I0755768

Sex, Lies and Sabotage

Sex, Lies and Sabotage

FROM RELATIONSHIP SABOTAGE...
TO RELATIONSHIP TRANSFORMATION!

The Secret to Creating Successful
Healthy Relationships!

Pamela M. Zimmer, Ph.D.

Published by GODDESS CALLING in 2009.
143-28 84th Avenue, Briarwood, New York 11435

Originally published as an electronic book in 2007.
sexliesandsabotage.com

A Note to the Reader
This publication provides the author's opinion in regard to the subject matter contained herein. Neither the publisher nor the author intends, with this publication, to render legal, medical, psychological, or other professional advice. With regard to any of these matters, the publisher and author recommend that the reader seek the advice of an appropriately licensed professional.

The publisher and author disclaim any personal liability, both tangible and intangible, loss or risk incurred as a consequence of the use and application, either directly or indirectly, of any advice, information or methods presented herein.

ISBN 978-0-578-01078-6

Printed in the United States of America

TESTIMONIALS

"I accredit all my recent success to Pamela. She is the only person who could teach me how to know myself and love myself. Our discussions have enabled me to realize my inner truth. I recognize things about myself now that I would never have known before... things that I love! Fear and anxiety are gone. Now that I know who I am, and moreover accept who I am, I have been able to flourish as an independent woman. Inner peace has arrived. Dr. Pamela has made me see my inner goddess and I will never ignore or suppress her again.

"I now feel great about my external relationships as well – with my family and friends. Also, my boyfriend and I have never known such compatibility until I met Pamela. We connect on a much deeper level now. Pamela opened up my eyes to so many mistakes women and men make unknowingly in their relationships. Most can be easily avoided – if you know what to look for. Pamela can help you with that. My boyfriend and I are now both getting what we want out of our relationship with each other and we have never been happier.

"Thank you Pamela."

- Jennifer Flannery

"Before I met Pamela, I used to allow myself to be emotionally tied to everyone and everything, out of fear of losing that person and/or situation. As a result, I lost myself. By the time I came to Pamela, I was a complete wreck. It was a long road but Dr. Pamela helped me to find myself again.

"She has an easy down to earth manner and a sense of humor that will make you laugh on your darkest days. She never gave up on me, and I wasn't easy. I resisted every step of the way.

"I had built up so many defenses and was so emotionally tied up inside I couldn't see clearly, and no one could see me... but Pamela could."

- Jazmin Ruotolo

"I had always believed relationships were about taking care of the other person and what their needs were, always above mine. Pamela showed me, through her own experiences, that every relationship is actually a reflection of you! So it's never about the other person, it's always about me! I couldn't understand this at first, because I never even considered my needs or desires when it came to relationships. How could it possibly be about me?

"But Pamela has a wonderful way of explaining things and helping you to see things in a totally different way. And she somehow manages to make you laugh through your own tears. The fact that Pamela shared so much of herself and her own life with me made me think maybe this might work, so I started doing what she said, and putting myself first, and treating myself in the loving, supportive way that I had treated others, and things started to change. There is not one relationship in my life that has not been radically transformed all because I started treating myself better. I mean WOW! Who knew this stuff really works! Thanks Pamela! You are truly amazing at what you do!"

- Carolyn Luna

"From the very start, Pamela has worked with me on helping me to better understand myself as an individual and to gradually learn to fit into my own skin and love the woman that I am. She has fully supported me in this process with the right amount of nurturing and insight. Pamela has guided me in recognizing how to take responsibility for my place in this world.

"Thru the years, with Pamela's guidance, I've been able to see more clearly the role I've played in my relationships with men... how the men I chose to become involved with had more to do with reflections of how I actually saw myself... and the type of men I attracted as a result. Because Pamela has helped me to see that, I can make better choices that are in my best interests and that come from a loving place within myself."

- Marilyn Mineo

"When I met Pamela, I was in one of a series of unhealthy, dysfunctional relationships, because of an unhealthy relationship with my Self. Pamela helped me to take my life into my own hands - to understand that I am not a victim of what happens to me, but I actually choose what happens to me.

"Having the knowledge and being conscious of that power, MY power, changed my life. She helped me to express my deeply suppressed anger and disappointments that I unconsciously held onto throughout my life, which had blocked me from my true potential.

"She helped me build my self-esteem – my relationship with my Self, thereby building the healthy relationships I now have with men, women, my friends, family, and the one man I call my husband, soul-mate, and biggest opportunity for further growth. I have never been happier. I am very grateful to have found a person that truly has the best interests of her clients in mind and heart.

"Thank you Pamela!"

- Lucie Lamster

"One way Pamela has really helped me is in the way I view myself today. Before, I didn't really think in terms of me being 'empowered' in my relationships with men. Without consciously being aware of it, I operated as if men had the power, so I in turn put men 'above' me without realizing it. One of the first things Pamela said to me when we started our sessions together was not to put men on a pedestal, that they are not above you. At first, when she said that, I thought, 'Well, of course not, I don't do that.' But as we got deeper in our sessions, I realized that, by not feeling like I had any real power in my relationships with men, I was in fact putting them above me and operating as if they had all the power. I came to realize that my relationships are only going to thrive if I feel empowered. But I learned from Pamela it has to be real. I can't just say it and think it. I have to start truly empowering myself.

"You have to feel the truth of it in your heart and soul. That's where real change comes from, and that's what Pamela helps you get at. Because in order to have healthy relationships, every part of you has to believe you can help create them, and if some part of you doesn't believe it, Pamela is gifted in helping you become aware of your own internal blocks to start unblocking and freeing yourself.

"Pamela helped me to 'get' how it's not about being good, or bad, but being whole and working with and accepting all the different parts of myself, so that I could begin to have a healthier relationship with myself, and that automatically helped with all of my other relationships."

- Liisa Lunden

"When I first met Pamela, to put it mildly, I hated men. I didn't realize this at the time. Then, I blamed them for being such losers. I remember Pamela used to cringe at the stories I would tell about how badly I treated them, but my heart was so closed, I didn't see it myself. I thought it was all on them. I didn't see that I literally beat them into being losers. Then Pamela completely blew my mind when she told me her take on relationships. She basically put all the responsibility on me. She told me how men live for us, and they can only go as far as we let them. She showed me that the anger I had at them was really with myself. I believed I was unlovable and any man who had the nerve to love me was going down. I was terrified of love itself! Pamela helped me release the anger and the heartbreak underneath all that rage. She's very brave. I had some very dark, scary moments and she stayed with me.

"Pamela knows when to hold your hand and she knows when you need to find your own way. Now I not only have the courage to allow someone else to love me, I have the courage and the privilege of loving me myself. Pamela, you are the brightest of the bright, and I think you have more wisdom then even you know!

"Thank you for being you!"

- Daria Kitano

"I started seeing Pamela when I was in a relationship and things were not going well. I knew that some of the problems stemmed from issues I had not resolved from childhood. She was able to help me figure out why I was doing the things I did that were sabotaging my situation. At times, I was reluctant to believe that maybe I was creating the problems myself.

"That was definitely a hard thing to realize. Of course, I wanted to blame someone else but I realized that I can only change myself. I continued my therapy sessions and I began to feel better. Pamela helped me to become more aware of my actions and to better understand them and I began to take steps to improve my situation. It hasn't always been easy but, with her help, I get a different perspective on the situation. This allows me to approach things differently. She has given me tools that I can use when I am in my head for too long. I still have challenging moments but at least I know I have Pamela to go to for help when I am in a crisis. She is amazing. Her wisdom and knowledge are one of a kind."

- Susie Rabines

"I've known Pamela for years. She has seen me through many ups and downs. Pamela has always been there for me with her loving support – when I fell, when I rose up, and when I hit a plateau. The amazing part is that she never judged me; she just accepted me where I was at each point in time. I felt true unconditional love and real acceptance coming from her always. Wow!

"I've learned through my connections with men that the most important person I have to connect with is my Self. When I don't honor me, in fact, I allow others, and especially men, to dishonor me as well. It's as if they follow my lead and learn from me how to treat me. Who knew?

"I am now at a place in my life where my career is taking off, I am beginning to make lots of money and, best of all, I am loving my Self. I can see how this love within me is my True Power and how it automatically emanates to others. When it comes to men, I am actually

in the process of creating that ideal soul partner connection and relationship within my Self first. Then, through the Law of Attraction, I'll be able to draw into my life exactly what I desire with clarity and bring that desire into full manifestation.

"Thanks to Pamela, I am feeling fulfilled without an actual man in my life, so that, when the time is right, I won't need him to complete me. I'll only desire him to complement and enhance my life. YAY TO EMOTIONAL INDEPENDENCE! YAY TO CONTINUAL EVOLVEMENT! YAY TO SELF-LOVE! YAY TO ME! YAY TO PAMELA!

"THANK GODDESS SHE'S HERE!"

- Alana Karagianakis

DEDICATION

I dedicate this book to the first and most significant woman in my life, my Mom. Her support for me has been unwavering. She has learned over the years how to fully demonstrate her love for me, and I have reciprocated with all of my love for her. We have cried together; we have laughed together. We have felt joy and sorrow together. Throughout, she has been there to listen, receive, and, when needed, give her advice. She has been my mother, my daughter, my sister, and my best friend. Through the many crises of life, the strength of our connection has endured. In fact, she refers to me as "the Light in her life." She believes in me and trusts me even when she doesn't quite understand. She has shown me, with rock-solid faith, that she knows that I have the power and the potential to go all the way towards the fulfillment of my dreams. It is for all these reasons, and so many more, that I dedicate this book, designed to show women the path of evolvement, to my very special Mom with all the Love in my heart and all the Light in my soul.

CONTENTS

INTRODUCTION

RELATIONSHIP SABOTAGE...
How and Why Women Do It!

Yikes! From this part of what was once the working title, you may be thinking that I'm blaming women for the current state of their relationships! While I'm not actually blaming women, I am holding them responsible. Why? The answer is because women contain the key that would not only help them transform themselves, but would have the added benefit of changing their relationships as well! In other words, women hold the secret to creating successful relationships with themselves and with others... and that's true power!

I'm Dr. Pamela M. Zimmer, a psychospiritual therapist, an intuitive, and a metaphysical healer. I founded the Human Relations Center for Women in 1989 and have worked mainly with women ever since, helping them grow and evolve – spiritually, mentally, and emotionally. Psychospiritual therapy is soul-based psychotherapy combined with spiritual counseling, relying on intuitive insight and knowledge of universal laws along with the use of basic psychological precepts. Karmic ties and belief systems can explain how and why we find ourselves in difficult situations.

Over the years, I have encountered every issue you can imagine that might affect women everywhere and anywhere.

The area that I most often encounter as the most painfully challenging for all women is their relationships with men. In fact, I've seen many women, who lived their lives in a very intact manner, i.e., successful in their careers, enjoying their female friendships, independent in their ways, come tumbling down once a man enters the picture. WHY?!

By the way, I am not only an expert in this area because of my professional knowledge, my spiritual understanding and my intuitive abilities, I also contain the insights and understandings gained through my own personal experience which fortunately, or unfortunately, depending on how you look at it, allows me to empathize with all women who are now going through their own relationship drama, or have in the past, or intend to at some point in the future. The mightiest among us seem to fall, or fail, when it comes to that which we believe should be second nature to us... our relationship with a man whom we love, or, at least, think we do!

But no longer do you have to fall, or fail, or go it alone. No longer do you have to battle alone in the dark groping for some meaning, or a way out. No longer do you have to engage in a seemingly endless cycle of self-sabotage. FINALLY, you will now be provided with the ANSWERS you've been seeking, the TRUTH you're yearning for, and the SECRET to a healthy and successful relationship. Join me as I unlock the key to the manifestation of your deepest desires for LOVE, HAPPINESS, SECURITY and INNER PEACE!

* * *

CHAPTER I

Why In The World Would I Sabotage My Relationship?

Well, that's a very good question! Believe it or not, there are many valuable answers to that question. Some may satisfy you, some may irritate the hell out of you, some may feel absolutely spot-on right, others may seem completely wrong. You may be aware of some of what I'm about to tell you, or it may all come as a total surprise that you could possibly be operating in such a manner that is completely oppositional to that which you claim, to yourself and/or others, you truly desire.

Certain explanations may come straight out of your conscious awareness, while others may be buried deep in your subconscious, set there long ago by conditioned beliefs or karmic ties to certain patterns, or even karmic connections. You may be engaging in certain behaviors purposefully and others habitually. It's time to discover just where you are coming from and exactly where you are going as long as you remain on your current path. Having fun so far?

Why do we make it all so complicated? Isn't loving someone supposed to be natural and easy… even joyful? I say YES! However, in order to get to the version of love we truly and deeply most desire, despite our efforts to the contrary, we first have to spend some time and energy examining what we are doing, feeling, and experiencing that is actually preventing us from being in a state of happiness in our relationships.

FEAR OF ABANDONMENT

The most common and basic fear that grips most women in their relationships is the fear of abandonment. You will all go to great lengths to avoid the possibility of being abandoned by your guy. Unfortunately, the very things you do to try to prevent this from happening are the very things that will probably bring it about. Sometimes, you just want to make sure that you never feel the pain associated with abandonment, so you keep yourself nice and detached and disconnected. The only problem with this is that you end up not feeling much of anything else either! Also, when you're feeling disconnected from the person you're in a relationship with and yet remain in that relationship, you ultimately end up disconnected from yourself as well. No fun there!

Abandonment, and the ensuing fear, has pretty much been embedded in us since the beginning of time. Most of you can trace it back to the very first man that abandoned you in this life – either physically or emotionally. In the majority of cases, that man would be your biological father. Now, we don't have to make this very psychoanalytical but, no doubt, if you give it some thought, you will come to realize that you may still be working out your unresolved father issues with your significant other. In fact, you can think of your so-called significant other as your significant issue!

Now I know you all understand physical abandonment, but let me just explain a bit what I mean by emotional abandonment. When a man is not in touch with his feelings and is actually scared of his own emotions, his tendency will be to deny you yours. This creates a distance and a disconnection. You then begin to feel that you are not being accepted for who you are, and you could even start feeling that your state of being is irrelevant and unacceptable. In other words, you either make yourself wrong, or you make him wrong, or both. Either way, a chasm has been created that becomes very difficult, or nearly impossible to cross. Eventually, you lose your desire to even try.

If it was your father who created this emotional distance with you, chances are you're walking around thinking that if a guy was to know the real you, he wouldn't like what he sees. After all, isn't that the message that your father gave you by making you feel ashamed or wrong for your emotional states? So now you don't fully value yourself, and wonder why anyone else would… *How dare a man claim to like, or Heaven forbid, love me! He must not really be seeing who I am! Or he must not be very bright or astute. I guess the problem is that I've been too nice. Now I'm going to have to show him just what I'm really about. Then he'll leave me for sure! In fact, it will be a good test. If he goes away, well, isn't that exactly what I thought would happen anyway. See… I was right! But if he stays after I show him just how ugly I can be, that must mean he really loves me!*

Oh, but not necessarily. Don't forget – you're with a guy who brought his own baggage to the table. He might stay, or go, for all sorts of reasons. There is no foolproof method for making him stay, if he needs to go. Of course, if he does go, you can always convince yourself that you were right in the first place. *See, he really didn't care for me, like he said he did. Otherwise, he would never have left me!* Again maybe, maybe not! The real point is that you actually left yourself! Therein lies the real abandonment. In fact, no one else can actually abandon you if you never abandon yourself!

Oh, tell me more. You mean there's a way to prevent abandonment forever? YES... and it entails you learning how to always be there for you. You must become your own best friend; you must give yourself the love you desire from another; you must stay connected to your True Self at all times. In fact, the Love you truly desire and continue to seek outside of yourself is actually contained inside your very being, waiting to be explored and embraced by you. Once you ignite this internal love, you can't help but share it with others, and then you will naturally draw to yourself those who are in alignment with you.

When you know how to love yourself and how that makes you feel inside, you will be unwilling to accept less than that from a man... and then you will know the difference! You must value your total self if you expect to be totally valued by someone else, at least on a long-term basis. But as I said before, it is necessary first to review and reflect upon those patterns that you continue to engage in that make you the grand saboteur of your love life!

CHAPTER II

Common Modes of Sabotage

I've noticed that there are several common threads which run through most unhealthy and unsuccessful relationships. These tendencies prevent you from having a growth-oriented dynamic relationship with your guy and keep you stuck in a holding pattern that eventually sends you into a downward spiral of misery and heartache. You are left feeling and believing that relationships cause tremendous pain and you begin to wonder if any of it is worth it after all. Well, I'm able to bring you some good news here. It is worth it and it does all serve a purpose. I will explain more about why and how as we go along... but first we have to deal with the bad news. Yuck!

UNREALISTIC EXPECTATIONS

I can't tell you how many of you set yourselves up from the start by placing false or unrealistic expectations on your partner. I can tell you that this mode of operation is pervasive and that I have been privy to a refusal on the part of many women to accept the potential destructiveness of this practice. In fact, in their denial, these women have vehemently objected to relinquishing their belief that they have the right to place expectations on another. When you place these internal and/or external demands which are based on your own personal expectations on your guy, you are basically saying two things: [1] I want you to do for me what I am unwilling to do for myself, and [2] You better do this for me, or else!

These expectations that become demands actually prevent you from knowing or receiving the real truth of what your man has to offer. You're now thinking that you wouldn't want to take a chance to find out what that is, because then you'd probably get nothing! Well, that may be so... but then, at least, you would know exactly what kind of man you're dealing with, and how much or how little he genuinely wants to give to you. And I say that that is worth knowing!

If you're imposing your expectations on your partner, his actions may be based on giving in to what you want from him, rather than on him finding his own authentic way to be with you. While this idea may not sound so bad to you, I assure you it turns out to be, in that, ultimately, it doesn't work in your favor. Why? Because then you'll never know if and when your guy is acting in alignment with his true feelings and intentions. This often leads to a lack of trust, an arousal of suspicions, and a severe breach in the integrity of the relationship. In other words, you are no longer experiencing the *true* him and disconnection occurs between you.

Example of Unrealistic Expectations

Although whenever the subject of marriage came up, Alice's boyfriend was very clear in his not wanting to entertain it, Alice continued to insist that, since they had been together for three years, it was time for them to "tie the knot." She ignored his protestations to the contrary and took matters into her own hands. She actually started planning their wedding, all without his approval or agreement. She felt that he would come around if he really loved her. She didn't believe that he wasn't ready or willing. Whenever he spoke against what she was doing, she made him wrong and disregarded his thoughts and feelings since they were not in alignment with hers. Needless to say, they did ***not*** *get married. However, they continue to live in misery together!*

* * *

CONTROL

Any of you women out there who need to control your relationship, or your guy, are doing so because you feel so *out* of control inside yourself, and/or in your life. The more out of control you feel, the more you believe it is necessary to make sure you stay *in* control of the situation, or the person, or the relationship. Where does this need to control your relationship come from? Insecurity! You believe that if you don't do everything in your power to take charge and run the show, you will lose... your man, your way, and your desired relationship. But guess what? Unless you have found a guy that wants to be dominated and told what to do every step of the way, and I really hope this isn't what you're looking for, your very attempt to control the way things go will lead to them eventually going completely the opposite way! Work on taking charge of your own life, and not someone else's, and you will get much further with your relationship.

An Extreme Example of Control

Whenever Betty goes out with her husband, she feels compelled to tell him what to wear, who to talk to, who not to talk to, and basically how to be in every way in order to make her look good. When he doesn't behave accordingly, she simply stops talking to him, until he comes around to her way of seeing things. For the most part, he goes along with this due to his own feelings of insecurity, but secretly carries resentment for her. After all, she never does let him show up! This is because she is afraid that, if he does, it is she who will lose control!

* * *

NEEDINESS

This is a fun one! Once again, the more you feel you need your man, the more you're expecting him to fill in for you where you have left off for yourself. What does that mean? In other words, when you find yourself needing more and more attention in whatever form you demand it, you are demonstrating your own inability to be there for yourself. The problem with neediness is that if it's met with the attention you crave, your neediness gets reinforced. It then doesn't have a chance to ease up and relax. On the contrary, like an untamed beast, it just gets stronger and requires more frequent feeding.

Anytime your neediness isn't fed, it turns into a state of desperation, which literally puts you in hell. You then become completely pathetic and are practically groveling on the ground in the hope of receiving just a crumb. In fact, you are so bad off at this point that a crumb will actually appear to you as an entire loaf of bread, and you will accept it eagerly and with much appreciation. This is one of the most painful cycles you can be in, and I strongly suggest if you find yourself here, you quickly find your way out! Trust me when I tell you... No woman belongs down here in this dark, seemingly Godforsaken place for long. Although I'm sure most of us, myself included, have spent at least a minute in this position, I strongly suggest that you find your way out of this abyss as quickly as possible. This may be where a therapist is needed for intervention.

Illustration of Neediness

Carol felt that, if she didn't see her guy every night, she would just die! One night, he insisted that he had to spend some time with his friends. She lost her mind! She called him throughout the night begging him to come over. He calmly told her that he would see her tomorrow night and that he was sure she would be fine till then. She swore she wouldn't be. This went on for a while. Finally, he couldn't take it anymore, and he came over to see her. Carol was so overcome by her emotions to see him that she cried in desperate relief. Of course, you now know that this reinforced Carol's anxiety and she continues to act out whenever the situation presents itself. She's stuck in her pattern of neediness and any co-dependent tendencies on the part of her boyfriend certainly do not help the matter!

* * *

ADDICTIVE BEHAVIORS

Any behaviors you find yourself engaging in repeatedly that always lead to negative outcomes, and yet you can't seem to stop yourself from repeating them nonetheless, are addictive behaviors. I've often compared what many women are doing in their relationships to drug addictions. People who take drugs do so for the initial high, and yet find themselves afterwards feeling worse than they did in the first place, which compels them to take the drug again in order to recapture the original high. Whether they do or not, they continue to feel the need to always strive for that outcome, even though they realize, at least subconsciously, that they will be left feeling worse afterwards. It becomes a never-ending cycle of insanity.

Well, the same thing happens in your relationships. You feel compelled to keep repeating the same self-destructive behaviors, getting the same negative results, and yet telling yourself that this time it may turn out differently. And you overanalyze everything, often staying stuck in your head. If you step outside of yourself for a moment and observe the action taking place, you will realize just how insane this really is!

Inside The Addicted Mind

He said something to me that I found quite confusing. What do you think he means by that? I'm going to email him and question him about it. It's been three days and he hasn't emailed me back. What do you think that means? I haven't seen him in a few days now. I don't understand what's going on.

Why are you so concerned?

In the beginning, when you're in the honeymoon stage, you get used to spending a lot of time together and you start feeling attached. Then when there's a day or two of separation, you feel lost, as if he doesn't want to be with you anymore.

So how do I not freak out when I have all these crazy thoughts in my mind? He doesn't want me. He's probably with someone else. Let me call him a million times to make sure he is where he said he would be. I have to ask him a ton of questions to find out why he doesn't want to be with me. Is it something I did? Is it something I said?

And the mental chaos goes on and on! No peace of mind here! But then again, my purpose for writing this is first to point out how crazy we frequently get in the pursuit of our love interests, and then to help free you from that insanity… which brings me to my next point of contention.

* * *

FALLING IN LOVE!

Who decided that the feeling of being in love should involve some kind of falling?

For your information, we are all born with two innate fears: the fear of falling and the fear of loud noises. Isn't that interesting that one of our most basic fears gets associated somehow with love? I also want to point out that love and fear are opposites. They both can't exist in the same place. So it seems that this world set us up for doom, gloom, and failure by pairing the notion of a fearful state with that of a godly one. Don't you find that strange and paradoxical?

While you may experience euphoria in that initial quantum leap into love, I say that, rather than falling, the real feeling could and should be best described by *flying in love* or *soaring in love* or *evolving in love.* Pick one. Take your choice. See how much better these terms fit and feel to depict that glorious state of allowing yourself to fully connect with another human being – spiritually, mentally, emotionally, physically, and energetically.

Then when the dust settles, you can experience simply *being in love!* So, stop your falling tendencies, which, by the way, usually lead to a downward spiral of emotional chaos and loss, and start thinking about love, in all of its myriad forms, as a place to grow from, to evolve from, and even to soar from. Whee!

And now on to the next scenario...

* * *

EMOTIONAL DEPENDENCY

Are you waiting by the phone for him to call? Do you postpone or even cancel other plans just so you don't miss the possibility of him calling to see you? Are you forgetting about your friends in the process... the friends that will still be there for you after he's not? If he does call, are you deliriously happy? If he doesn't call, are you completely messed up emotionally? Are you actually staring at the phone willing it to ring and praying that it's him? If someone other than the guy calls, are you disappointed, maybe even upset? Are you obsessively thinking about him, him and you, you and him, night and day, day and night?

Well, you get the idea. If you are in a "he can make me or break me" mode, you are most definitely emotionally dependent on him. This state leaves you often feeling like a victim who is frequently at the mercy of your perpetrator! But there is no crime being committed here. In fact, in this rather common form of self-sabotage, the only one committing a crime is YOU, on yourself! You have set yourself up to totally rely on his actions and responses to you to determine your minute by minute state of being.

Now that doesn't seem fair to you or him. You are, in essence, making him responsible for you, your feelings, your well-being, your emotions, your happiness, your sadness, and your reactions based on those emotions. You're teaching him through your ways that he can literally *make you or break you.* You're showing him that you are not strong on your own, that you're emotionally weak, and need him to make you feel good about yourself.

In fact, what you're actually doing is giving him all your power to use over you, and then you're saying, "Please be gentle with me. I am so fragile. Please don't hurt me. If you do, I will blame you for everything. After all, I did give you the full responsibility to take care of me and keep me happy."

Okay, I know you're not actually saying these very words to your guy, but this is what your intention is and this is what he can gather from your actions and reactions towards him. What's worse is that you're teaching him that emotional dependency is the way to go in relationships!

An Emotionally Dependent Woman

Rhonda literally loves or hates her boyfriend based on what he has shown her that day. If he's been good to her and given her what she wants, she will tell you how wonderful and strong their connection is and how much they love each other. However, if you hear from Rhonda on a bad day, one in which her guy did not come through for her in some way, she will go to the other extreme, expressing her misery and her desire to just end it now. It's like being on a roller coaster! You never know what you're going to encounter with all of her reactive upward swings and downward spirals. Her state of being and feeling is totally dependent on what he does or doesn't do, and she is always in a reactive mode!

* * *

I don't know about you, but this doesn't sound like the powerful independent woman I desire to be. Perhaps you are recognizing yourself here. If so, I'm sure you don't like what you're seeing. But remember, for those who are personally fed up with these old patterns, there are remedies coming up for all of these delightful forms of self-sabotage, whether they be conscious or unconscious. So hang in there!

* * *

APPROACH-AVOIDANCE

Are you the type of woman that believes you know what you want and like in a man and you go after it when you see it... only to find yourself caught in the grip of fear of actually having to have a relationship once you're there? This is an interesting dynamic in which you approach with confidence, and once you have attained the man's interest in return, the avoidance part of the cycle begins. This is a form of protection that you will often see played out by men who like the chase but fear the intimacy. Well, it turns out that there are some women who run this same cycle.

Basically, what you're avoiding is the possibility of being hurt, of being seen for who you really are, of being loved, of letting someone in to a place that you have kept well-hidden for a long time. You enjoy getting the guy but not what comes after. Of course, this does appear to be a game that you're playing, but you and I know better! Each time you make your approach, you want to believe that it will be different now, that you will be different somehow. So in some ways, it surprises you as much as it does your partner, when you're suddenly no longer either emotionally or physically available. Taken to the extreme, you avoid him like the plague!

There is something in you that just doesn't feel safe being that intimate with anyone. In fact, the only way you can hold on to your autonomy and your tough exterior is to make sure no one ever gets close enough to see what's beneath the armor. The intimacy you fear, by the way, has nothing to do with sex... if only it were that simple! Rather, I'm talking about the kind of intimacy where you get to open up to another person and reveal yourself and let them in. And that, quite frankly, frightens the living daylights out of you!

This seems like the opposite of emotional dependence, doesn't it? But, in fact, you, too, are nowhere near emotionally free. The difference is that, in this case, your emotions are completely locked up. You're a prisoner inside yourself. This is a state you believe you have to maintain in order to stay strong. You most likely believe that any show of emotions is a sign of weakness when, in your case, the opposite might actually be true! Your internal block of ice is going to have to melt in order for you to have a genuine loving connection with a man. Ew, scary, right?

Living In Approach-Avoidance Mode

Denise met a guy in her office building where she works. Everyday, she would see him when they both showed up at the coffee cart. At first, she would just smile at him. Then she began to greet him with more and more friendliness. They started having small conversations that became more extensive over a short period of time. She thought she had nothing to lose so, one day, she asked him out. He happily agreed. After going on several dates, an internal voice started sounding an alarm telling her to "Get out now!" She knew she had to end this with him before it went much further. She felt that she couldn't risk that possibility, so she literally started avoiding him. She stopped showing up at the coffee cart and she stopped answering his phone calls. If he tried to come see her at her desk, she would dodge into the bathroom. Finally, after many failed attempts on his part, he gave up. And Denise was relieved! "Must avoid intimacy at all costs," she told herself in so many words!

* * *

I remind you, once again, that there are solutions to all of these forms of self-sabotage. But it is important that you first start recognizing yourself and your tendencies and what you do to keep your man at bay or completely lose yourself to him and/or make him responsible for your entire world.

Remember, many years ago, when Helen Reddy sang those powerful words, "I AM WOMAN... HEAR ME ROAR!" She was certainly onto something that is important to all women everywhere. While you don't have to go around roaring like a lion in order to claim your womanhood, you do have to start expressing your Truth in all situations and particularly in your relationships. If you don't, you end up denying your Self, settling for very little, and becoming less and less of Who You Truly Are. Eventually, there's not much left to work with. You've lost your most valuable commodity... YOU!

This brings me to another diminutive form of self-sabotage...

* * *

SELF-DENIAL

This category will challenge what most of you have been told and have been raised to believe in regard to how to be with a man, how to keep a man, how to please a man, and how to make sure you don't end up alone. I hate to be the bearer of bad news but, if you've been taught to deny yourself in any way in order to hold on to a man, it will be absolutely necessary for you to unlearn this most erroneous teaching. And the self-denial I'm alluding to even includes compromise!

Every time you lie about who you are in a relationship, you are denying yourself. If you start a relationship by "putting your best foot forward," and showing the guy only the qualities that you believe he wants to see, you are denying yourself. For those who do this, I assure you that, at some point down the line, you are going to resent him for making you have to hold up your end of the bargain when, in truth, it was you who set it up that way to begin with. You essentially taught him how to see you, and now you're surprised that he expects that all the time. So now you're stuck with the very set-up that you created by not being honest in the first place!

When you are not honest in your responses, and don't express your true feelings, you are denying yourself. Even if it's for the sake of "keeping the peace" when you're not at peace within, you're denying yourself. When you make yourself matter so little, guess what your mate is going to do with that? You got it! He's going to behave as if you matter so little. Remember always that you teach people how to treat you. Then when you go into agreement with how they perceive you, you further reinforce that state of self-denial.

This then becomes a vicious cycle whereby you keep repeating the same self-denying behaviors and you continue to receive the same inconsiderate and thoughtless treatment. The only way out is to find the way to break this pattern that is so detrimental to your personal welfare and your self-esteem. More on that to come.

An Illustration of Self-Denial

Elizabeth was brought up to believe that the woman takes care of the house and cooks the meals for her man. So, when she married at the age of 21, this was exactly what she did every day. Although she accepted this role, it does begin to wear thin when you are doing this day in and day out. In addition, Elizabeth provided ongoing support and continual encouragement for her husband in regard to his business. And, of course, over time, instead of receiving appreciation for her efforts, she was taken for granted.

One day, Elizabeth was out with a girlfriend enjoying herself when she suddenly realized the time. "I have to get home to prepare dinner for my husband," she told her friend. "I must go now." Her friend, who was single at the time, was annoyed by this, and told her so. She adamantly tried to convince Elizabeth that she was wrong for leaving, and that she shouldn't go. Now maybe Elizabeth's friend meant well, but her tactics were harsh and controlling, so Elizabeth was upset by this. Nonetheless, she went home to do what she had intended in the first place.

The reason this exemplifies self-denial is that Elizabeth was not able to give herself permission to stay out and have fun on this rare occasion, because she could not break out of her conditioned role to be free enough to do so. She denied the part of herself that wanted to continue her enjoyable outing and not be rushed due to a sense of obligation. Although this is just a small illustration, over the years, Elizabeth continued to deny her many talents and desires and stayed stuck in a pattern that she herself had set up. Always being taken for granted and rarely being appreciated led to a build-up of resentment in her that, to this day, she is still trying to work her way out of.

* * *

Unfortunately, this is all too common amongst women whereby they deny themselves and their truth and, instead, opt for losing themselves in their relationship. Often this is done to the point where you no longer even know what your truth is because you've hidden it from yourself for so long. When you deny your Self, you invite others to deny you as well. Certainly, you can't expect your man to support your true Self when you have stopped supporting her yourself a long time ago, if, indeed, you ever did!

* * *

DRAMA QUEEN

I feel compelled to include this as one of the self-sabotage categories since I've seen so many women engage in this tactic in their relationships. If you are a so-called "drama queen," you tend to make mountains out of molehills. You take things out of context and twist them in such a way to serve your need to create drama where none might have existed. Why do you do this? For the attention, of course!

The problem worsens when you don't care if the attention is positive or negative, but just that you're being paid attention to on a regular basis. So you resort to all sorts of antics, even making up stuff, just to force your mate to listen to you. You'll even drag your friends into your sideshow in an effort to get them into agreement with you, not caring whether you're actually right or wrong.

You just want to be taken seriously, and you'll go to great lengths to assure yourself of this. Frequently, you're more than a bit over the top in your presentation. However, when you continually engage in this behavior, your partner will actually stop taking you seriously and will inevitably start tuning you out. So, in fact, for all your efforts, you actually end up with the opposite of what you thought you wanted and believed you needed. No attention, but plenty of dramatic stories to tell. Now if only you could get someone to listen, or even care!

A Drama Queen Named Helen

Helen was out having a festive dinner in a waterside restaurant with her husband and a group of friends. Throughout the meal, she made sure to capture most of the attention by conversing in an animated fashion with everyone at the long table. Directing most of what was said, asking questions with feigned interest, and laughing on cue, she ran the show as the center of attraction. At the end of the meal, after the bill was presented, her friends put in their share and left the table.

Only Helen, her husband and two guests remained. Helen's husband, who sat at the opposite end of the long table, apparently said something that did not sit right with Helen. Well, she opened up her mouth and quite literally roared like a lion! She did not care that her other friends were privy to this exchange, or that other diners in the restaurant could hear her. She embellished and exaggerated to make her point well beyond what the actual situation called for. She took no prisoners, and did *not show one ounce of regret for her extreme actions. This indeed was her show and she was going to dramatize to the nth degree, thinking that she was one hundred percent right every step of the way!*

* * *

LACK OF WORTHINESS

I am not worthy! I am not worthy! I am not worthy! Time to self-flagellate! If this describes you, you find yourself constantly questioning your partner's motive for being with you in the first place, the second place, the third place... well, you get the idea.

What does he see in me? Why does he like me? Why does he claim to love me? I am not worthy of him, or his love. I don't know what he's doing with me. I'm sure it's just a matter of time before he realizes that he made a huge mistake. Then he'll tell me the real truth! Of course, what he tells me at that point, I will believe. After all, my lack of self-worth makes it clear to me that

I don't actually deserve true happiness or somebody to love me. I certainly don't see what there is to love, so how could he!

I know that what I'm characterizing sounds awful, but it's not as uncommon as you may think. Many women are walking around out there appearing fine on the outside while they are tearing themselves to shreds on the inside. Self-worth is a valuable asset, and in order for you to ever be truly happy and attain real love, you must acquire it. Often, your conditioning has led you to believe the worst about yourself and made you feel that you are truly undeserving of anything better.

This state of unworthiness translates itself into your relationship in the form of self-doubt and disbelief in any expressed feeling towards you, and eventually leads to mistrust in your partner. This is your baggage to unpack and sort through on your own, or with the help of a professional therapist. To impose this on your guy will just lead to your worst nightmare coming true and your unworthiness will then feel totally justified.

Feelings of Unworthiness

Jackie had this to say after being married for five years and discovering that her husband had cheated on her: "I just don't think a woman can ever forget or feel like enough to her husband after this. Even in the midst of feeling confident about herself as a woman – not beating herself up, but still not feeling like you are enough for this specific man."

* * *

JUST A NOTE

It may seem as if some of the above categories of behavior patterns are similar, or that they overlap, or even blend together. This is not by accident. They do, in fact, share many commonalities. Often, when you engage in one mode of self-sabotage that leads to the sabotage of your relationship, you also take on the characteristics of other closely related forms. While this is common, and even seems natural, most of you would agree that this is not the desired state of being that you want to continue creating over and over again. And yet, despite yourself, the cycle does get repeated!

* * *

CHAPTER III

A Case Study – Susie's Story

Susie is a young, attractive, intelligent, professional woman who appears to be emotionally intact, calm and friendly in her approach to people, and a good listener. In fact, she is actually the "go to" person for her friends when they are seeking advice, and she is able to deliver. This describes Susie when she is not in a relationship with someone of the opposite sex.

Susie is actually a client of mine and has agreed to share her story in order to help other women who might identify with her and some of the phases she has gone through as well as some of the positions she has put herself in. She is currently successfully navigating her way through a relationship that she's in by doing the work on herself that frees her from her former patterns.

I decided that, in order to get the most out of this format, Susie and I would sit down together and I would essentially interview her about certain events in her life that have contributed to her issues with men and relationships. This way, I could present a good picture of what has led her to where she is now and what she has figured out since. So here now is her story...

Tell me about the first significant man in your life.

My father... Very strict man, not easy to talk to, set in his ways. Nothing you ever did was good enough for him.

And what affect did that have on you?

That's what made me feel very insecure. I developed a lot of fears because of it. I never really felt good about myself.

What fears did you have because of his impact on you?

I think I feared everything. Not really believing that I could accomplish anything in life so I never took any chances. I used to participate in a lot of activities as a young child, but then when I became an adolescent, it felt as if something had died in me, as if the light within had gone out. And I always questioned, "What happened?" I struggled in school and everything just went downhill from around 7th grade on.

How do you think your father affected your view of men?

My father was always a great provider who took care of his family financially. He made sure we had a roof over our heads, food on the table... but you could never really talk to him. He encouraged us to tell him stuff but then when you did, if he didn't like what he was hearing, he would start screaming and yelling. So eventually I learned not to even bother. Because of that, it became increasingly difficult for me to open up to men. If a feeling was being stirred up in me or there was something I needed to talk about in later relationships, I would suppress it. My feelings would continually be suppressed because I didn't feel safe expressing them. Then they would build up to the point where they no longer could be contained and I would explode with rage.

How else did your father impact your life and your way to approach men?

My father was unfaithful to my mother, something I was always aware of. At the age of 9, my mother told me that she wanted to leave my dad, and I was devastated and I begged her not to. So she stayed. I was relieved. However, later on, in my teen years, I felt guilty and wondered why she had listened to me back then. Had she not, it would have saved us years of emotional abuse, mental abuse, and constantly living with the fear of not knowing when he was going to release his rage on all of us again. Real torture! It was so bad that I used to pray that he would die on his way home from work... just to prevent him from returning home again only to lash out at my mother. It's made me feel very strongly that I will never put up with that kind of treatment from any man ever!

His betrayal of my mother with another woman created in me a sense of mistrust and doubt in men. In later relationships that I had, I often found myself waiting and wondering when the guy that I was with was going to cheat on me. This led to great bouts of jealousy which I expressed by constantly questioning everything they did. I needed details in order to be convinced that they were telling me the truth.

Tell me about the first relationship you had with a guy in which you began to realize just how your father's behavior did impact you.

At 23, I was introduced to a really nice guy that swept me off my feet. (*Well, that's a red flag right there! See my topic entitled "Falling in Love."*) It was very intense and full speed ahead. At first, we were able to talk about anything and everything. But, as time went on, things began to change. Suddenly, the very notion of him going to hang out with his friends and not spending all of his time with me would arouse my jealousy. I would express my jealous feelings, but not in a nice way. This would lead to arguments, which I would win often, and that resulted in the buildup of resentment in him. However, it created a sense of power in me. So I would use that power to constantly enforce my rules. But eventually it all backfired!

Months and months of constant questioning, nagging, and demanding answers on my part finally led to a great outburst and emotional breakdown on his part. We were driving in the car and having some disagreement related to my jealousy issues, when he suddenly screamed at me, "I FRICKIN' LOVE YOU! I don't understand why you don't believe me." I was speechless and actually felt afraid because of how he broke down. I thought to myself, "What the hell am I doing? Oh, my God! This guy really does love me." I then understood that all of this frustration was coming out of him because I didn't believe him or trust him.

Although I saw the negative impact that my jealousy and mistrust were having on him, I was not able to completely stop myself from going that way. I did, however, greatly reduce my need to question everything from a place of doubt. After a while, I thought things were going much better between us. I knew he had real feelings for me, but I was to discover that, unfortunately, the damage was done, and he had not fully recovered from it. The toll this took on him eventually led him into the arms of another woman. And I was left wondering why in the world I had sabotaged this relationship, but also what I did to deserve this outcome!

How did you spend your time in regard to men following that relationship?

I dated a couple of guys after that, but nothing serious. Although I met some guys, it never really went anywhere. I guess my wall was up, and the moment I thought this may be leading in the direction of a serious relationship, I found myself running in the opposite direction. Wow, there were actually a few guys that this happened with. I was too afraid to get hurt again... the pain was too fresh.

This went on for several years. In one situation, it was a casual relationship, but we did become sexually intimate. And even though I knew that he wasn't someone I could see myself with, I started developing feelings for him. When I observed him flirting with other girls, I would question him about that. That's when I realized that my jealousy had reared its ugly head again! Then we would end up sleeping together. Following that, I would become detached by telling myself that we were just friends.

This became a repetitive cycle, until we finally parted as friends.

Were you aware of this pattern in yourself at the time which kept you from forming truly intimate relationships?

I really didn't know what was going on with me at the time. I created confusion for myself by not knowing what I really wanted. I just wanted to have fun and developed several crushes along those lines. However, when I started feeling something for this one guy, I thought maybe I do want something more. But in the process of playing that out, I came to realize that I hadn't fully worked out my issues and they were still showing up unexpectedly, and tripping me up. That's when I prayed to God to keep me single!

And did that work for you?

It sure did. At that point, it did keep me safe and able to do what I needed to do in my life. I didn't have to deal with the emotional roller coaster that I felt relationships were for me. I pretty much was okay with being single. Because of what was going on in my life at that time, I felt that a relationship would be more than I could handle. I wasn't sure if it would be good or if it would be bad, and I didn't want to risk finding out.

What, if anything, happened to change that point of view?

Things were getting better in my professional life and the direction that my career was going in. And I finally felt like I really wanted to start dating. So then I asked God if He would just please send me someone nice, not that he would have to be "the one." Just send me a selection and then I'll choose when the time is right. In the meanwhile, I'll have a lovely assortment of men to date!

But that was not to be the case! I went out with a nice guy but we just did not click. However, that gave me hope that there are at least some nice guys out there. And then, a couple of months later, I met another one. And I still had it in my mind that I just want to have fun so we will see where this goes. But, as life would have it, he turned out to be special for me. And I found myself pleasantly surprised at what I was feeling for him, even though I had only known him for a short time.

I found myself wanting to open up to him immediately. I was aware of that, but at the same time did not want to rush into anything too soon. So I made sure that I kept that wall there to prevent my emotions from overcoming me. We developed a nice connection and I was trying to learn how to live in the moment. Then when I realized that my feelings were becoming stronger for him along with the more time we spent together, that's when my insecurities started to come out.

How did your insecurities manifest and how did they affect the dynamic of the relationship?

I began to question his actions, and it created tension in the relationship. I found myself wanting to know all that this relationship was about right now. This need in me created anxiety. I was afraid to get hurt again, so I needed to find out where this was going for me. All these unanswered questions rolling around in my head led me into a fearful state, which made me feel even more anxious about the possibility of being hurt. It became a vicious cycle. I was concerned about whether I could really trust this person and open myself up to him. He seemed so sincere, but I didn't know for sure if that was the case.

The tension that this created between us led to us both being very cautious and unsure of each other. But at least we had good communication with each other so we were still both willing to talk things out and figure out where things were going for us.

What insights did my counseling provide you with?

That's when I realized that I want to be in a relationship in which I am emotionally independent, and that I have to focus on the connection between us and not get caught up in the attachment. I have to start letting go of my fears of getting hurt, so I don't keep recreating the old pattern in my new relationship. I have to trust that I'll be okay whichever way it goes. If it ends tomorrow, I'll be hurt but, ultimately, I know I'll be okay.

So then what happened?

For a while, I drove myself so crazy that I knew that I couldn't go on much longer in that manner. I needed to find the way out of my emotional turmoil and the chaotic thoughts in my head. If I didn't, I knew that I would drive away any chance of allowing this relationship to work. However, I also had a part of me that was telling me to just cut my losses and walk away. And remember that fun that I wanted to be having... yeah, I wasn't having it!

So then I was determined to make changes. I knew that we really did have a connection, so I started focusing on that, which led me to begin to trust it. That helped lessen the questions of doubt in my mind and freed me from some of the attachment that I previously had which compelled me to need to know what the relationship was about.

Tell me more about your ego attachment.

My ego attachment led me to want to make sure that he wasn't deceiving me and that I was always one step ahead of him. Or so I thought! This attachment, however, kept me uncomfortable and mistrusting with a continual need to question everything. My head was filled with obsessive thoughts that kept me in a constant state of uncertainty. I felt like I needed all the answers from him. I didn't realize at the time that all that I need to know is inside of me. So it was a continual struggle for clarity… and I was losing!

How did you begin to overcome this?

I then started focusing on the feelings I had that were in my heart, rather than the thoughts that were stuck in my head. This helped me feel connected to myself which in turn allowed me to feel the connection I had with him. As long as I came from my heart and stayed out of my head, I was alright. I started to relax and trust the present situation and what was there for me now. When thoughts came into my head to disrupt my flow, I pushed them away by not engaging with them, and thereby avoided creating an entire scenario of negative possibilities.

Through this process, I helped myself get more and more in touch with my own truth and my own feelings. Little by little, I freed myself from some of my conditioned beliefs and habitual ways of thinking which really were no longer working for me. I realized that in some ways I had been addicted to operating the way that I was in relationships, and needed to stay on top of the steps I was now taking to become consciously aware of what was really true for me and what I now desired to believe. Where I had been feeling somewhat dependent on his behavior and his reactions, I now started taking my power back by taking responsibility for my own behavior and reactions. By doing so, I began to feel more and more emotionally independent along with a sense of freedom.

It certainly sounds like you've made a lot of progress.

While I am still a work in progress in terms of my relationship, both with myself and with my boyfriend, I am no longer experiencing all the craziness I had been. Things are a lot calmer within me and, therefore, outside of me as well. I am now able to approach situations that arise between us by first examining my own motives and seeing my purpose and knowing my intentions beforehand so that I am then discussing it with him with a clear head. When I take this approach, I am very happy to report that I derive a much better outcome. In fact, we both benefit by the mutual exchange of our individual viewpoints and, as a result, my new state of emotional independence is reinforced and I am supported on my path of growth and evolvement.

CHAPTER IV

Relationship Dynamics

We now need to explore some important relationship dynamics that take place in almost every partnership you form, which can often create a dichotomy, or split, in your feelings, as well as the feelings of your mate, that leaves you more confused than ever about what's really going on. Here now are the most common dynamics you will encounter in your relationships.

* * *

REFLECTION vs. PROJECTION

This dynamic literally goes on in every relationship you have. According to the Law of Attraction, you draw people into your lives that are going to reflect back to you where you're at, whether you like it or not. In fact, you're usually drawn to the person who will bring up your issues, forcing you to deal with them or deny them. But take heart... you can attain tremendous healing through these often crucial entanglements; that is, of course, if you don't go into denial!

This naturally includes the men you choose to partner up with. You can often figure out stuff about yourself by what you see reflected back to you from the other. That is, of course, if you are open to the idea that you are actually looking into a mirror of yourself on some level when you are noticing the image of your mate.

Reflection is a wonderful tool if you use it as such. It's often easier to observe certain aspects in someone you are relating to than it is to be aware of them in yourself.

Now, the aspects you might notice may be desirable or undesirable. If you like what you see, then you will realize that this is a part of you that may already be pronounced or, if not, then it likely lives as a potential within you that you can consciously develop now that you've come to admire it in another. In fact, whenever you do feel admiration for a particular quality in someone else that is not yet developed in you, know that it probably exists in a potential state within you. Now that's cool!

The flip side of that same coin rears its ugly head when you don't like what you see reflected back to you and you judge it negatively. Now, of course, in this case, you are being given the opportunity to change this state of being within yourself. However, that is not what most of you resort to as your first inclination. Here's where the state of reflection turns into projection.

You tend to engage in the dynamic of projection when you make a negative judgment against a particular behavior that you feel you cannot accept in your partner. The truth is it's a quality that you actually find unacceptable in yourself, but refuse, at that point anyway, to see it as having anything whatsoever to do with you or your ways. It is much easier to believe that this belongs solely to him than to believe that you contain such an irritating quality. For instance, if you accuse your guy of being ungenerous, that quality exists somewhere in you in some form, hidden or obvious. It may not manifest itself in the same way it does in him but nonetheless it lurks within you. Yuck! Right?

The problem with projection is that things start getting confusing because the real truth about the ownership of the behavior or attribute in question is ambiguous. Whoever is doing the projecting feels that he or she is on the high road, and it is the other that needs to change. Now, is everything that you dislike in the other a projection? Not necessarily.

I've discovered that the key to realizing whether you are projecting or not is this. After you throw your fireball, get in touch with what your real truth is. In other words, what are you actually feeling around this sentiment that you have expressed? If you only feel contempt and destructive criticism for this aspect in your partner, there's some projection going on in you. Bear in mind that you also may be projecting a quality on your guy that belongs to a previous boyfriend or husband and not to the present one. Tricky, eh? If, on the other hand, you simply feel that a situation could be improved with some awareness that comes about through constructive criticism, then it is more likely not a quality in you, or a previous lover, that you're projecting onto him.

Now, interestingly, projection can also be used by you in regard to an admirable quality in the other that you are jealous of because you don't realize that you, too, contain at least the potential to develop that attribute. In this case, you may find yourself being sarcastic in your approach. For example, you may make remarks such as: "You think you're so great because..." or "Just because you're good at such and such doesn't mean that...!" These comments are usually thrown at the other person because of your own feeling of inadequacy in that area. So you hurl some venom in order to put down any good feeling your mate may have about himself in that way. In essence, you are trying to take it away from him. After all, if you can't have it, why should anyone else?

If you could instead just allow yourself to be aware in each situation when you are reflecting and when you are projecting, you have the ability to learn volumes about yourself as well as about your guy. This is one of the ongoing dances that takes place throughout your relationship. It's up to you whether you make it a waltz, a tango, the mashed potatoes, or the jerk! Salsa, anyone?

* * *

CONNECTION vs. ATTACHMENT

This is a really interesting dynamic and one in which I find myself having to often remind the women I'm addressing to remember. Basically, connection is healthy; attachment is unhealthy. Connection is soul-based and spiritually oriented; attachment is ego-based and physically or materially oriented. Connection leads to feelings that come from the heart and grow; attachment causes emotions to be expressed from your ego self in a state of desperation. Connection leads to independence and interdependence in a relationship; attachment leads to emotional dependence and co-dependency in a relationship. So... connection, good; attachment, bad!

When you meet someone and you feel an energy exchange between you and him, this is your soul telling you that there's a connection here. Now, a connection does not mean that you must have a relationship with this person. Sometimes, the purpose of the connection is served simply by saying hello, or smiling, or even just walking by. I know a lot of you will have trouble with this concept. Most women ask that if there's a true connection, doesn't that mean I'm supposed to have a real relationship with this guy? The answer is "No." It doesn't mean that you're supposed to, but it doesn't mean that you're not supposed to either. Confused yet?

Every person that we connect with serves some purpose to us whether they remain in our lives or not. It is up to us to either figure out the purpose and thereby understand what role that man could play in our lives, or simply acknowledge that there is a purpose and act accordingly. What does that mean?

If you believe that you have met someone with whom you have a connection, that either means that you have come together to complete some unfinished business from a past life, if you can accept such a concept, or heal some aspect of yourself from this life. It could also mean that by having a relationship with this guy, you will be taught many lessons that you have come here to learn, or that through your connection with this man, you will grow and evolve in order to become even more of who you really are. In other words, his impact on you will bring out those qualities or assets in you that will transform you in some significant way. And, of course, it may turn out that this is the very connection that elevates you to a state of *being in love*.

All of these and so much more are valid bases of connection for your relationships to flourish and/or for you to gain from them. But now here comes the down side... *attachment!* Often, you come together with someone that you're attracted to and feel the energy surge between you that I referred to earlier and decide to take steps towards creating a relationship. Fabulous... until your issues kick in, that is!

Insecurity, low self-esteem, unworthiness, fear of abandonment, fear of rejection, mistrust, jealousy, possessiveness, and/or need to control may be some of your possible issues, along with whatever else you can think of that has the effect of scaring you into no longer trusting the connection. Once you believe that you have to take measures to keep your guy with you, you have crossed the line from the fun world of connection into the fearful and worrisome world of attachment! Congratulations!

Unfortunately, once you cross this line, your worst states of emotionality begin to get felt and expressed. Your relationship then becomes for you a living nightmare, one in which you rarely wake up from, at least not without the aid of a wake-up call. Attachment makes you feel out of control all the time. You have moved into your own version of hell. You are constantly relying on your partner to not only do right by you according to your rigid standards of right, but you find it intolerable to your state of well-being when he doesn't. You are forever vigilant to make sure that he walks the straight and narrow so you won't have to suffer even more.

Doesn't that sound like fun? And yet it's a place most of us have spent some time in. Why? Why would we inflict such punishment on ourselves? Well, the simple answer is that although your soul may be satisfied with the connection, your ego has decided not so much! Your ego works through you as your voice of doubt and stirs up feelings of fear that lead you to taking action that you otherwise would not have. To put it bluntly, attachment messes you up emotionally. And unfortunately, your ego is all about attachment! In fact, your ego thrives on attachment, much to your chagrin.

Whenever you are coming from fear or doubt, you are in essence feeding your ego. I suggest that you stop for a moment and request that your ego-self joins your soul-self in sharing in the celebration of your connections, and tell your ego-self that you will provide a place for her if she behaves well and agrees to align herself with your Truth, your Higher Self, your Soul Self. If you can get your ego-self to listen, you can then relax and enjoy your connection from a place of love rather than having to effort to maintain your attachment from a place of fear.

To sum it up, connection leads to healthy soul-based love in which you come from your heart. When you remain connected with your soul-self or Higher Self, you naturally attain a state of self-love which allows you to emanate loving energy to your partner and also helps you to recognize when you are receiving true love. On the other hand, attachment leads to unhealthy ego-based love in which you come from fear and doubt. When you remain in this state, you actually disconnect, not only from your mate but from your True Self as well. In this condition, you cannot recognize whether you are receiving true love because you certainly are not reflecting it!

* * *

POINT OF INTEREST

Don't mistake sexual and/or physical attraction with soul connection. Although you may have an actual connection with the man you're physically attracted to, you also may not. When chemistry is at play, it is often confusing as to whether you have an energy dynamic with this person beyond sexuality or physicality or even physiology, for that matter. If you start off with a chemical reaction, I suggest that you get in touch with yourself internally to see if there is also a spiritual or soul connection being activated as well. Otherwise, you may think you really desire a relationship with this man when all you really crave is a sexual rendezvous because you find him so appealing. Good in bed does not necessarily equal good to wed! True intimacy is an energy exchange way beyond physical sex. Decide what you're seeking in advance in order to determine the correct direction for you to go in this regard.

* * *

HEART-BASED DESIRE vs. FEAR-BASED NEED

When you come from your heart, you are coming from a place of self-love. Therefore, any desires that originate in your heart center are connected to your Higher Truth. Love for yourself surrounds these desires and they are expressed by you with purity of heart and mind. You are not looking to impose them on your partner or control him with them. They are an emanation of what is true for you and, as long as these desires and your love remain heart-based, you can't go wrong. In fact, you will always be guided by your Higher Self because you and your actions are in alignment with your highest good.

However, an unfortunate dynamic often develops when your heart-based desires aren't realized, and you begin to doubt your mate, or even blame him for not coming through for you. As soon as doubt or blame enters the picture, you have moved into the realm of fear. It is at this point where your previous desires now begin to be expressed as fear-based needs. You start to believe that only the other person can bring you what you need and that, if he doesn't, you will not attain it otherwise and you will be sadly lacking.

Of course, anytime you are coming from fear, you have disconnected from your soul-self and your ego has taken over. With your ego in charge, you are no longer able to tap in on your heart connection, and you end up spending most of your time residing in your head. You begin to feel dependent and desperate because now you're not able to express your true love for yourself or for your guy. This is a lonely scary place to be because, like a child, you are now living in a world where you are totally at the mercy of someone else to meet your needs. Whether your partner does or does not is not the question, nor is it the solution. In point of fact, even if he does, your state of fear will not subside; rather, it will grow stronger.

Anytime you get your fear-based needs met, it is actually your fear and doubt and insecurity that get reinforced. In fact, you begin to feel that the only way you will get what you claim you want is by remaining in a fearful state. Of course, you are not likely to be conscious of this, but nonetheless, the fear takes over and ends up controlling your life.

The only way to free yourself from remaining in this position where all your needs and demands are being expressed through fear and uncertainty is to step back and find your way once again to your heart center. Once you manage to arrive, be still and feel compassion for yourself. Vow to stay in your heart so that you can continue to love and provide for yourself all your desires. In this way, you have now opened your heart to receive that which your mate truly wants to give. When you remain in a state of self-giving and self-loving, you naturally draw to yourself the same from others.

* * *

THE DANCE OF LOVE?

The final dynamic I will allude to here is one in which almost every couple engages. I'm calling it the Dance of Love although I'm sure to most of you, it often seems like it has very little to do with love. But I assure you that, whether love is present or not, you will do yourself a great service to learn the steps of this dance. It will save you much anguish and grief if you do.

You take one step forward... he takes two steps back! You then take two more steps forward. He then takes four steps back! You continue taking four steps forward. Then what happens? He leaves the room, hangs up the phone, doesn't call you for a few days, and generally finds ways to avoid you. What kind of dance is that? Certainly not one I care to engage in! With this method of movement, you end up dancing alone!

My recommendation... instead of pushing, always create space for you and your partner. What does that mean? Well, when you take a couple of steps forward and he begins to step back, you may entertain two options. One is to stand still. The other is to step back as well. Standing still allows him to feel that you are at least acknowledging his need to withdraw momentarily. Stepping back as your response actually has the effect of creating space for both of you. It gives you the chance to get centered and relate to yourself. It gives him the opportunity to now take the initiative because you have removed the feeling of imposition on him that he was experiencing. So it's a win-win situation when you provide energetic or emotional space. And by the way, *only women can create space.* Men have to rely on women to do so. Since this rarely happens, that is why men often feel the need to flee, physically or emotionally.

* * *

CHAPTER V

Solutions That Lead To Relationship Transformation

Here I will be presenting those main areas that, if processed and worked upon, will lead you to the highest state of gratification you can attain within a healthy relationship. Oh, yes… and you'll have a truly healthy relationship… not only with your guy, but with yourself as well. Can I get a YAY!!! Now pay close attention…

* * *

EMOTIONAL INDEPENDENCE

This is the platinum gold path and the final frontier to ultimate freedom! When you attain Emotional Independence, you are fully in touch with your real and genuine feelings and your authentic Truth, while you are free of your emotionality and your reactive emotional states. Imagine if you could experience your relationship without ever being at the mercy of your captive emotions again. This means that you would no longer be the emotional affect of what your partner does or doesn't do. You would be free to choose and decide what you want to feel. *Your happiness would not be determined by someone else.* You would totally be responsible for your own feelings and would no longer be reacting to his.

Responsibility actually is the ability to respond in all situations... respond, not react. There's a big difference. When you respond, you come from a place in which your feelings are in alignment with your Truth. When you react, your ego is running the show and your emotionality gets the better of you. In fact, in this case, you have actually given your power to your mate by inadvertently telling him that his whims are controlling you. Who wants that? Nobody, right? Well, then, why is it that most women have linked their very happiness up with what their man decides to do or not do?

Most of you strive for physical and material independence so that you can manage your lives without having to rely on someone else to take care of your every need. Some of you strive for spiritual and mental independence so you can be free of conditioned beliefs and come to your own conclusions. However, when it comes to Emotional Independence... well, it seems like the majority of you believe that you're supposed to be emotionally affected by others, and that they need to change or treat you in a certain way for you to feel okay.

I cannot stress the following point enough. *When you make someone else responsible for your feeling state of being, you are giving them power over you.* And what's worse is that it is your own power that you have given away so recklessly. And, to add insult to injury, it is likely being used to manipulate you by the very person you've handed it to! Please, please, please, take your power back with the understanding that only you are responsible for how you feel.

You want to learn to express your true feelings without acting out your emotionality with your mate. I strongly suggest that you find ways to release your raw emotions when you're alone so that you can clear the way for what you are really feeling to come through. That way, you can honestly and rationally explain what you are emotionally feeling without losing control.

By demonstrating Emotional Independence in your relationship, you actually become a role model for your guy to follow as well. Believe it or not, men tend to be even more emotionally dependent on women than the other way around. Women just make it appear as if this is not so! So you will be providing a healthy model by going this way. And we do want healthy partnerships... right, ladies? And besides, Emotional Independence leads to a healthy interdependence in the ideal relationship in which you dynamically rely on each other without losing your individuality and without becoming co-dependent.

* * *

SOUL CONNECTION AND HEART-BASED LOVE

When you draw someone into your life through spiritual and metaphysical energy, i.e., through the Law of Attraction, please honor the fact that you do have a soul connection with this person. According to Dr. Wayne Dyer, "Manifesting is not about getting things that are not here. It is about attracting what is already here and is a part of you on a spiritual level... What I am seeking is seeking me." That means that a greater purpose will be served by your coming together in some way.

However, it doesn't necessarily mean that this will be a long-term relationship, or the be-all to end-all of relationships, but it does signify that you have something to gain here that is important. It may be a life lesson that you need to learn; it may be your development in a particular area in your life; it may be your chance to express and release painful feelings; it may be your opportunity to learn more about yourself; it may be an experience that teaches you more about love.

Also, bear in mind that you are often drawn to the person whom you most need in your life at that particular time in order to heal yourself through that connection. In such a case, he will actually bring up your issues, directly or inadvertently, forcing you to deal with them. Know that the process of allowing yourself to re-experience old pain enables you to release that pain. So, much growth can take place.

By acknowledging and honoring the connection, your soul thrives and you grow. In fact, the more you keep any ego-attachment out of the picture, along with any major resistance, the more you will evolve and benefit from everything that this relationship is there to show you. And, of course, it will be a mutual benefit for both you and your partner because soul connections cannot be one-sided. So, although you may find staying connected without becoming attached in any sort of dependency a real challenge, I can assure you that it will be worth it to you to do so. And the relationship will actually flow in unexpected ways!

Heart-based Love is the state of connection you want to attain. In this way, your heart remains open and you are actually receiving what you are giving simultaneously. The more you allow love to flow from your heart, the more love you will experience for yourself as well. Only when your love comes from your heart and soul is it true and authentic. When this is not the source of your love, you are likely expressing fear-based feelings that disguise themselves as love.

How do you tell the difference? Heart-based love feels really, really good deep inside of you. Your heart is open and full. Fear-based "love" always leaves you feeling empty and anxious. Your heart is closed and you are scared to open it. But because so many women create entire relationships based on these feelings of fear, it is very common to believe that you are experiencing real love. The problem is, at that point, you just don't know the difference!

Once again, your ego is doing the speaking and feeling for you, and it's very good at deceiving you in this way. So check in with yourself from time to time to see if you can discern the difference inside of you. By staying in the moment and living in the present, you can gain clarity about whether you're experiencing love or fear. Where one is, the other one isn't, by the way. So get out of your head and go to your heart and soul for the real answers! And know that you contain all the answers you need within you.

* * *

BE TRUE TO YOUR SELF

Bear in mind that all the information I've provided here is not designed to make you subservient to the man in your life, but rather to empower you with the responsibility to fully live your Truth and to completely embrace yourself with Love. Being true to yourself means that you will naturally be true in what you express in your relationship. It is actually a state of being that you can attain when you decide that you will no longer dishonor or degrade or deny or downplay who you truly are. When you are true to yourself, you are centered in your honest feelings. And it follows that when you are true to your Self, you can't help but be true to others.

You give and receive from this place of honest truth. You live in integrity and wholeness and you do not compromise yourself in any way. In fact, when you compromise, it is not what most people think it is – a meeting in the middle, or halfway, in order to come to agreement. Compromise is actually a denial of your truth or, at least, a watering down of it. This does not mean that you have to become rigid in your position. It simply means that you must be sure when you agree to anything that you are still living true to yourself and not simply going along with the other person just to satisfy him. Never ever compromise your integrity or your values for anyone!

You must be careful not to betray yourself or your Truth and, thereby, settle for less than you are. Women, often in an effort to be nice, will easily go along with that which they are not in agreement with, just to avoid making waves. You can very nicely tell your partner how you really feel, revealing what is acceptable to you and what is not, and then allow him to do the same. You don't have to agree. You just have to allow Truth to be expressed so everybody gains in the end!

* * *

LOVE YOUR SELF FIRST

Everyday, look your Self straight on in the mirror, gaze deeply into your eyes, and say over and over again, *"I LOVE YOU."* If you do this daily for several minutes at a time, I assure you that you will begin to experience strange new feelings for yourself. You may find your face changing as you gaze upon your reflection. You may find your heart softening for and towards yourself. You may start feeling your own soul connection to your Higher Self. You just may start knowing Who You Truly Are!

If you do this practice at the beginning of your day, it will help you learn to be kinder to and gentler with yourself. I know that most of us find it easier to be kind to others, or even to complete strangers, than it is to be nice to ourselves.

But it is so important to begin this nurturing process now and start to love the person you see looking back at you.

The truth is that in order for you to attain the True Unconditional Love you really desire, you must first have acquired it for yourself. In fact, once you start loving yourself, your next level of evolvement will be to actually become the Love that you now are. You can then graduate to this next level by including another statement to your mirrored reflection. *"I AM LOVE. I AM LOVE. I AM LOVE."* You can alternate between *"I LOVE YOU"* and *"I AM LOVE"* and have a real epiphany!

* * *

CHAPTER VI

Q & A

This chapter will be a forum whereby I will endeavor to answer those relationship questions that have been presented to me by my clients and their friends. I will also be including what some women themselves had to say in lieu of asking any questions. It's all quite interesting and revealing to see what women are actually thinking and believing and accepting regarding the current status quo of relationships. So here we go!

* * *

Why must women always be the ones to take responsibility for the state of their relationship?

The short answer is that there would be very little hope of creating healthy relationships if women did not take charge and it was left up to men. In fact, if you observe any relationships where this is the case, you will see what I am talking about. This is not a condemnation of men, but rather an understanding that most men are operating so far from their own Truth and in such a disconnected state, that to let them take the lead when it comes to your relationship is a role that, frankly, they were not born to play nor are they prepared to do so!

Women, on the other hand, are much closer to their Truth and their spiritual essence and, if they will allow themselves to draw on that wisdom, free of their conditioned beliefs, they will be able to successfully lead and direct a progressively healthy relationship, with themselves as well as with their partners. This is the role that women were born to play! So I encourage you to connect with your Self and find your own answers within, as this will empower you. Then treat yourself with the same respect and tender loving care that you would desire from your mate. And by the way, men actually want to be shown the best way for them to be in relationships, that is, if it is done by modeling and not by dictating!

How do I allow myself as a woman to be vulnerable and draw strength from that?

In your vulnerability lies your strength. Do not equate being vulnerable with being weak. Rather, vulnerability is a state of openness in which you reveal and demonstrate that you have a heart and that you actually feel stuff. This is a good thing! This makes you human. You are showing trust for yourself and the situation that you're in. That alone makes you stronger, regardless of what responses you elicit because of it.

Is there such a thing as just having a physical relationship?

Sure, men do it all the time! In fact, when you are engaged on that level alone, you will actually feel like a man. Why? Because you have activated your male energy and disconnected from your feminine energy. Male energy is about doing and taking action. Female energy is about being still within and receiving. In fact, we were biologically constructed to demonstrate this very contrast. Masculine energy is an active and sometimes aggressive force, while feminine energy is a creative and receptive force.

This does not mean that women can't have sex without love. But it does mean that, when you do, you are operating in a detached mode, cut off from your heart and soul, void of feelings. Your genitals are doing the talking, so to speak! This should also help you understand better what men are experiencing, or not experiencing, when they continually go this way. Not only do you objectify your partner, but you also go into agreement that this low level of relating is acceptable and sufficient. By doing this, you're actually perpetuating the opposite of what the majority of you women claim you desire – *true love and real connection!*

Interestingly, I recently heard a guy on television, who was talking about the dating scene, declare that, "Ultimately, we're all animals!" Unfortunately, that may have been the case up till now. But the truth is we were put on this Earth to be more than that. In fact, we were actually created to be human beings! Go figure! I say that it is time that we started rising to the occasion, making new conscious choices, and ascending into our true and evolved state of humanness. That way, our precious earth creatures can lay claim to the title of animal and continue to enjoy the benefits of their God-given nature.

Okay, let me step down from my soapbox now!

Why do women settle? Why don't they hold out for exactly what they want?

Fear and insecurity. Low self-worth. Low self-esteem. Women are afraid that if they don't accept what or who has presented himself in their lives, that no one else will come along. So they might as well not take that chance! Or they're thinking that maybe this is the best that they can do. Most women do not believe in their Soul's ability and their Higher Truth to draw in more appropriate connections which would serve a greater purpose in their lives. Your human mind has been conditioned to believe that you are not worthy of your many gifts.

Many women tell me that they'd rather be with the wrong man than be alone. Sad but true! If you truly loved your Self, you could never take this position. In fact, it would be to the contrary. Then, you'd rather be alone than be with the wrong man! But, unfortunately, too many of you still believe that you must settle for what shows up rather than create your own desired reality. Sometimes, based on our experience, we start adjusting our picture of what love is supposed to look like just to keep from having to change our present situation. Often, maintaining the status quo in your relationship is more appealing and less scary than making any changes.

There's also the conditioning factor. All too frequently, family and society promote the idea that it is more important to be married than to be happy with your Self. Many people even look down upon being single, with the implication that something must be wrong with you. So you're going to have to find the strength within to stand up and take a position which supports your true desires, even without the agreement of loved ones, or society at large. And remember, to settle means that you don't value your Self and what you're really worthy of attaining.

How do I live in the moment in my relationship?

By remembering that *the present is a gift you give yourself.* When you dwell in the past, you often repeat the same old patterns over and over again, since that is where your attention and your focus takes you. So mistakes that you've made in previous relationships will tend to get played out in your current relationship, even though the dynamics might be different. But, by bringing your baggage into it and unpacking it for all to see, you simply set yourself up for the same doom and gloom that you previously encountered.

When you move into the future with your thinking, you totally miss the point of what you are there to learn and experience in the present situation with your guy. You also tend to impose your future expectations on him, not taking into account that the steps to get to that future moment are not only necessary, but significant to your growth as an individual and as a couple. In essence, you devalue your relationship as it now exists by saying that you want it to go somewhere else that it isn't right now!

Also, women tend to project onto their mate their ideal version of him, neglecting to see who really stands before them. Often, it is his imagined potential that you are taking into account that, if realized, would make him the perfect man for you! Unfortunately, his potential may never be actualized, and then you are forced to choose between living for some future moment when he may, or may not, become your ideal, or moving back into the present and accepting him where he's at now. That may be where he remains... so love him or leave him!

How do I learn to trust a man?

By learning to trust your Self first! Real trust is truly self-trust. When you give your trust to a man, you are simply acknowledging the fact that you trust your Self enough to remain intact, regardless of which way this goes. You trust your intuition to guide you and you trust your instincts to alert you as to the best direction for you to take at each point of the relationship. You fully allow your stream of well-being to flow through you and to you continuously. You trust that your responses will always be in alignment with your Truth and that you will never betray your Self or deny your True Self.

Why don't women support each other but they will kill their firstborn to support their loser men?

Got to love that angry Aries energy! In all seriousness, though, women are led to believe that they're in a competition with each other, and guess what the prize is... a man! So rather than question the veracity of this current state of affairs, most women accept it and fight till the death to hold onto their man, even when he is a "loser" as you point out. They're holding onto conditioned beliefs that tell them that they must keep their man, at all costs. They do so at great expense and sacrifice to themselves, their loved ones, their friends, and all who might intervene in the nightmare that they choose to hold onto. They operate as victims and not as empowered women with their own voice and their own Truth.

The reality is that, for us to create a transformed world, women are going to have to come together as allies and as sisters, supporting each other and connecting on such a level as to bring about a total turnaround in these completely outmoded and false beliefs, which have consistently demeaned and oppressed women. Only when women understand that they only have to compete with themselves and that the only prize they need to compete for is to become the best version of Who They Are, will they then be able to support each other in realizing that potential. And, as we as women become actualized, we will lead the way for men to become "winners" as our equal partners. Amen!

Can a relationship continue, happily, after discovering that your man has cheated on you?

It depends on what the nature of his cheating is. In other words, if he is seeking comfort and solace in the arms of another woman because he doesn't feel like he's able to resolve some aspect of his relationship with you, then it is up to you if you want to do the work to mend your connection and bring peace between you. After that, if you are satisfied that he is now completely with you, and you are able to let go of the pain that you feel he has caused you, and forgive yourself for taking on so much of it, then you can go on together happily. But this is a choice you must make. Basically, you're deciding whether you can accept that what has happened is now over, that you have both learned from it so that it has served a purpose, and you feel secure in the knowledge that you are both now on the same page with moving forward.

However, if your guy is cheating on you because, well, that's just what he does, then that is his pattern and he has personal issues that belong to him and not you. Therefore, you don't have to take them on as if it's your problem to solve. Like an alcoholic who's addicted to drinking, your man is likely addicted to having affairs, and stopping will only occur when he decides to get help, or acknowledges that he even has a problem. In this case, unless you can live with the nature of such a man, happily, your best bet would be to leave and thereby restore your own sense of self-worth.

But the real questions you should be asking yourself are not, "Do I leave or do I stay?" or "Is he worth it or not?" but rather, "What does this relationship or situation teach me about myself, not about him, but about me? What is the lesson here for me? What is this here to teach me or to show me? What am I getting from this?"

Why do men cheat, plain and simple, especially after they are caught and seem to profess their love for you?

Again, it is likely that the men you refer to are locked into a holding pattern that compels them to repeatedly go after other women, usually for emotional reasons, even when sexual gratification is involved. Something in them does not feel complete where they are and they're looking for women to give them the self-assurance that they lack and to tell them that they're okay just the way they are. These men need their egos stroked, often along with other body parts, repeatedly! Of course, when they receive this attention, their pattern gets perpetuated and, like a bottomless pit, they need more and more.

I suggest, if you find yourself spending most of your time trying to figure him out, you are losing your Self in the process, and your time would be better spent in figuring out how to best serve you, your needs, and your desires. When you shift the focus off of him and put it on you,

you will find that your energy becomes more contained and you become clearer about what your true value is, and why you have been attracting this situation into your life. At that point, you will be able to make the best decision for yourself... out the door, no doubt!

Why does marriage seem like the woman is always giving and the man is always taking? Why do men feel like they need to take?

Likely because that is what's happening! The truth is that it's supposed to be the other way around. Male energy is giving and action-oriented and female energy is receptive, calm and still. Of course, we're all some combination of those two aspects to different degrees but, if you're a woman who is in touch with her feminine energy, your prevalent state would be open to receive, or receptive, and your man's predominant state would be actively giving. Surprise, surprise!

Unfortunately, women have been brought up to go against their basic receptive nature and become the givers. Men have been raised to receive from women and, if they have been taught, or have learned through modeling, to be aggressive towards women, then they feel entitled to take what they want. Even though this current set-up is out of whack and needs to be reversed, under no circumstances is it acceptable for a man to take from you! This implies that you are less than him, that you are somehow subservient to him and, if you allow this, you are perpetuating your own oppression.

In fact, women have the power to set their relationships up correctly from the beginning once they are armed with this knowledge and understand that it is truly your choice. You decide what you will accept and allow and what you won't. The best choice is a balanced give and receive relationship with no taking ever on either part!

Why do so many women fear disagreement/arguing with their man so much that they will sacrifice their beliefs/their truth just for the sake of not arguing? Why must we always play nice? And, why will we be the first one to pick up the phone/email, etc. and apologize??

Many women believe that if they disagree or argue with their man, they are causing a threat to the relationship. Obviously, it is more important to these women that they "keep the peace" and "play nice" rather than "rock the boat" and possibly produce consequences that are not desirable. Of course, there's a difference between arguing every petty point and actually standing up for what you truly believe in. When you deny your own Truth for the sake of not making waves, then you are sacrificing a part of your Self. This is dangerous because, if you do this enough times, there won't be much left of you!

You need to feel like you can express whatever you need to say to your partner and it will be okay, regardless of how he reacts. However, when it is something that really doesn't matter to you one way or another, then to create disagreement just for the sake of argument is not the most desirable way to go. If this is done frequently, then when you really want to be taken seriously, it is likely that your guy won't even be hearing what you're saying. So please choose your battles wisely!

As far as taking the initiative to apologize goes, this is good if you are coming from a place in which you are able to show that your ego has not been wounded by whatever the circumstance was, and you can be mature about it. But when you are apologizing simply out of the fear of possible loss if you don't, and the true loss is to your Self if you do, then this is not the best way to go. Sometimes, arguments and disagreements happen for you to learn something more about your Self and the particular relationship you're in, and you need to allow that without quickly wanting to sweep it under the rug just to avoid possible ramifications that you don't wish to encounter!

Why does it take women so long to open up after they have been badly hurt in a relationship? Why do they fear so much the thought of being hurt again?

Look, no one wants to be hurt ever, let alone again! So your ego, which creates the state of fear that you find yourself in as you embark on another relationship, screams in your head, "Warning, warning! Possible danger approaching! Avoid at all costs!" And whether you're consciously aware of this loud voice or not, the desired effect is achieved. You become overly cautious and fearfully take baby steps to move forward, if at all. It is likely that a huge wall has gone up inside of you that prevents you from really feeling much of anything. Unfortunately, this keeps you disconnected from the good stuff as well as from the painful stuff.

It's important to remember that, with a closed heart and your ego running the show, you will never be able to let in or express or even feel the kind of love that all of you yearn for. You remain detached from your emotions and disconnected from your true feelings. If you could tell your heart to open, it is true that you might experience some scary things, but the benefit of being able to feel love for your Self and others fully far outweighs this. So learn to trust your Self to know what's right for you at the time and begin to take some calculated risks.

Why do so many women give up THEIR friends after they get married, and spend almost every weekend double dating with their husband's friends – even when they don't really like them very much?

This ties in with the idea of women giving up their own lives, including their careers, their friends, and their ideals, and losing themselves in their husband's life. Many women feel that they must absorb themselves in the life and activities of their man in order to make sure that they are sufficiently involved and playing a significant role, so that they are a part of everything that goes on with him. So they do whatever they feel they have to in order to accommodate their man.

The truth is no one should have to give up anything that is really important to that person as an individual. But women must be willing to continue connecting with them Selves as individuals, and that may mean occasional independent activities. It is healthy to maintain ongoing relationships with your friends even after you are married. If these women were important to you before, why are you not willing to demonstrate that after the marriage?

When you spend time with his friends whom you do not really like, you are not valuing yourself enough to be honest. It is also possible that your husband does not see his friends for what or how they are and just accepts them carte blanch. This is fine for him, but when he's bringing someone new that he values into the picture, there's now a different dynamic to be considered... one which may not work for you as a couple!

Why will most women permit their man to criticize them privately with regard to their weight, cooking, housework, their family, their job/career? While he gets fat, lazy and comfortable??

Indeed! When women do not enter their relationship with high self-esteem, you reflect those feelings about yourself to your guy. He picks up on this, consciously or unconsciously, and if he is not someone interested in looking at himself and his own foibles, he will begin to criticize what he sees as yours. This is called *projection.* If you allow this, it is because of your own insecurities and self-doubt. As he continues to chip away at your so-called faults, you start to believe in what he is saying and you begin to allow those things to define you. You end up feeling so bad about yourself that you actually go into agreement with him against yourself.

Now, when you're both so busy denigrating you, it is difficult to take notice of the fact that he is the total loser who has grown fat, lazy and comfortable criticizing you! By criticizing you and putting you down, he has actually pumped himself up. He now appears to be the prize to both of you! I suggest that you get some good counseling to help you build your own self-esteem, and then you will see the truth of why the situation is in your life. Remember, the question always is, "Why did I attract this into my life?"

It is important to note that a woman has to know her boundaries and be clear about conveying them to her mate. That way, if your guy does start acting emotionally abusive towards you, you will know with certainty what is acceptable and what is unacceptable, and will be able to nip it in the bud.

Why do I seem to make all this free time for my man when he never fits me into his life?

Because somewhere in your conditioning, you have come to believe that when your man shows up, you'd better be available. Heaven forbid, he thinks you actually have other important things to attend to in your life!!! You fear that if you don't make the time for him at his beckoned call, that he may stop calling altogether! Guess what? If he does, then that means that he, too, places total importance on him, and there really wouldn't be enough room in his life for the both of you, anyway. Please don't tell him through your actions that you are less important than he is. Remember, you teach people how to treat you, so you can be sure, if you go that way, he will never make you a priority in his life!

Why do women drop their friends as soon as they get involved with a man?

Unfortunately, women feel that they have to place all of their attention and energy on the man that has shown up in their lives at that moment. He may be gone a moment later, but that doesn't seem to matter. After all, he's here now, right? Once again, through your actions, you are telling this guy that he is more important than any women in your life. This is not the message we want to continue relaying to men, but until you realize that your relationships with your female friends are just as meaningful and important, if not more, you will continue to make any man that comes along and shows interest in you the center of your life. After all, why not take your friends for granted? They'll still be there after he's gone... or will they?

I am a strong, confident female and I seek out strong confident men, but it seems only weak, passive-aggressive men are attracted to me. Why is it that strong females can't find strong men?

First of all, if you are strong and confident, I suggest that you stop seeking out and looking for men altogether. What I mean is the energy that you are exerting in your search may actually be attracting the very men you are not interested in. Weak men are drawn to strong women so that they can feel balanced by the contrast. In essence, you may be filling their need and neglecting your own. The fact that some of these men are passive-aggressive may indicate that they actually resent your strength because it is not theirs.

The way to attract men that you feel are strong is by being more self-contained in your strength and confidence and putting yourself in a more receptive position. This would then allow your energy to draw in more effortlessly that which is like you. Remember, *like attracts like.* But also be aware that there may be a lesson for you to learn even from the weak men. In fact, you always have to ask yourself, "Why did that show up in my life now?" Bear in mind, too, that there may not be many strong men around yet! Remember, we develop... then they develop.

* * *

SOME COMMENTS BY WOMEN

Here now are some thoughts and beliefs expressed in writing to me by some women. These comments, to my estimation, represent what a great deal of women are feeling, thinking and believing in regard to their current status in relation to men.

One woman had this to say:

We become so attached to men because they, in our minds, fulfill that VOID where we are lacking. Women, at times when they are not satisfied with their own lives, give everything to men hoping that it will make it all better when, in fact, most men only care about themselves and do not appreciate us.

Another said this:

Yes, boys are a topic that is greatly discussed, but remains a mystery (at least to me). Maybe it's because women are looking too deep. Women are complicated, beautiful creatures whereas men are just stupid and selfish. (If you note some bitterness, don't worry; I'm not aggressive, just weary of men's ignorance.)

We should look at men as we look at cars: most likely, it's been used; so if something is broken, don't bother fiddling with it, just replace it. When men are aware of the replacement factor, they are more likely to behave themselves. In the end, everyone wins... and by "everyone" I mean the women – and that's what matters!

And one said this:

I think that women that drop their friends when they get involved with a man do so out of lack of self-esteem. I think that they feel like they need to be available for the guy whenever he wants to see them out of fear that he will lose interest or find someone else to date if they can't see him. They feel that the friends will be there but who knows if the guy will stick around so they might as well see him whenever he wants to see them.

I think it is in a woman's nature to want to be in a secure relationship because we are nurturers and being in a relationship allows us to exercise that quality. So when a guy wants to be in a relationship, we latch on immediately and follow his lead. That is why women who follow "The Rules" really stand out – because most women do the opposite of "the rules" (using all their spare time to see the guy they are dating; and canceling plans with friends to go out with the guy at the last minute).

One of my clients said:

I'm beginning to understand that you can have a strong connection with a man, and yet not actually be involved in a physically present relationship. My niece had been experiencing exactly this with a man that she has known for eleven years. Circumstances prevented them from being together until recently, when their enduring connection brought about a physical reunion that resulted in their getting married. It's amazing to see just how powerful their union is. I guess mountains *can* be moved when the energy between two people is strong enough!

Another woman had all this to say:

I've been kind of turning something over in my mind. Why do we (women) worry so much about hurting our men, even if they don't worry about it, and even hurt us?

Since I've been thinking about this for a while, I have some ideas. I think it's harder for women to break up with someone who is going to be heartbroken, and I think our stakes are higher. I think women really value the idea of being needed, and if we convince ourselves that a man needs us, it makes it seem even crueler to leave him.

I know a woman who has been unhappy in her marriage for the past 15 years. He has mentally abused her; he is utterly cruel to her sometimes. She is sick now, and not only is he not looking after her; he aggravates her heart condition with stress. She is financially set for life; she is a strong, interesting, intelligent woman. She has friends and family who love her. Why will she not leave her husband? She has told me it's because he needs her!

* * *

Wow! Sad but, all too often, true! The song, *"What's Love Got To Do With It?"* by Tina Turner, comes to mind. So... *What's love got to do with it?* If the answer is, *"Nothing,"* then your next question ought to be, *"Why are you still there?"* Bear in mind that love and need are *not* the same thing!

* * *

MY FINAL COMMENTS

Although women can act quite smart and savvy, strong and intelligent, and speak in a very self-assured manner, it seems when it comes to relationships, all that goes out the window. Until women realize that they need to become emotionally independent and continue to evolve when they're partnered with a man, I'm afraid that the status quo will be maintained. Please realize that it is men who actually need us and not the other way around. We were just led to believe and buy into that myth so that this current reality would be perpetuated.

Know this... As much as it seems to still be a man's world, even men, in the depths of their souls, are hoping that women figure this all out and step up and take their true place and the lead role in their relationships. This way, men, too, will have a chance of coming into their own, following the lead of women, and not the other way around. And remember, we lead with female energy, which our planet has been without for way too long and is hungering for. Until we turn it all around, becoming who we truly are, and then helping men to become our equals and who they truly are, we will continue to be strangers in a foreign land where nobody is speaking the same language and we just keep raging on!

For now, know that Self-love without self-judgment will lead you to your desired outcome. Remember that life is a mirror reflecting back to you what you are emanating. So loving your Self will bring about an equal return. Let's bring True Love to our world by being the love we truly desire within our Selves!

* * *

CHAPTER VII

A Special Closing

When I'm in a relationship with a man that I love and find myself engaging in any self-sabotaging behaviors, aside from all the tools I naturally have at my disposal, what really helps me the most to make a rapid transition is Remembering Who I Really Am! By opening my heart and activating my soul's connection to the Universe, I'm able to put my faith in my Higher Power and fully trust in the process that will take me where I most need to be... a place of Self-Love and Self-Acceptance.

It is in that regard that I offer this gift to you in the form of the following letter, in the hope that you, too, will be able to Put Your Faith in the Universe (God, Goddess, the Oneness, the Light, Your Higher Power, or whatever you choose to believe in) and Trust in the Process that will bring you to your rightful place of Self-Love and Self-Acceptance.

> ***"What the caterpillar calls the end of the world, the master calls a butterfly."***
>
> — Richard Bach

When I allow my Soul to be in complete alignment with the Universe and fully connect with that energy in a state of Oneness, and totally open my heart, a powerful Divine Feminine energy force manifests itself in me. You might say that I become a channel for its expression.

I refer to this Divine potential that my Soul thus emanates as Mother Goddess energy because that is how I experience the nature of this powerful vibration. From this connection, I am able to see Divine Feminine energy in the Souls of all women;

thus, my use of the term 'Goddess' in the letter I am presenting to you here.

If you can allow your Self to open your heart to receive Her message to you which comes through my Highest Self, you will begin to feel the Love and the Light that lives in a potential state within you. With that said, please accept and receive this gift I offer to you now. Know that it comes from the Love in my Heart and the Light in my Soul...

* * *

My Dearest Daughters,

I write this letter to all women everywhere from a place in me that is filled with Universal Mother Goddess energy. From this Source within my Soul, I can see Who You Truly Are quite clearly. You might say that I can read your souls!

And what I see is brilliant! In fact, if you could all see the Truth of Who You Are, you would be overwhelmed with awe. You are all beautiful Goddesses each expressing different shades of Light and color in amazing and quite exquisite patterns. You are each unique and have something wonderful to offer the world and the planet.

Please know that you are all vehicles of Light who have come into a physical body in order to have a human experience. Your Soul Selves are the expression of your Higher Truth. At this time, it is very important that you begin to integrate your Soul Selves with your physical selves, so that you can start to live in alignment with who you are on the highest level and on the deepest level.

I tell you all this to lay the foundation for my wake-up call to you. You must stop denying your Selves. You must start realizing your worth and your worthiness. You must begin to comprehend the real spiritual power you contain. You must now understand that you are the prize, and you must acknowledge that Truth through all of your actions everyday.

When it comes to relationships, my dear ones, embrace your Selves with the Love that you are. This is the biggest secret of all... You actually not only contain, but truly are, the Love you desire. Please stop seeking it outside of your Selves, as if someone else is holding onto the gift that is yours. When you do that, you diminish your own Light and deny what is yours to Be and to emanate to others.

As your Universal Mother and Creator, you are all a part of me. And it most pains me when you continue to make choices that denigrate your beauty and magnificence. I know that the conditioning of this world, along with the extreme density, makes it difficult for most of you to find your way as true individuals, but I cannot stress enough how important it now is for you to step up and honor your birthright as the Princess Goddesses that you are.

Open your Hearts! Get out of your heads! Let the Light that is you be expressed in all of its glory. Choose to love your Self first and fully. Then, from there, choose to love that which reflects back to you the Love that You Are! Anything that does not will now show itself to be clearly out of alignment with your Higher Truth, and you will no longer wish to entertain it.

You all must become the role models for this new way of bringing True Love to our precious planet, Mother Earth. Your feminine energies will water Her and sustain Her. Imagine, if you will, an Evolution Revolution, where all women band together, empowered by their Truth as unique individuals, coming together in Oneness, fully supporting each other, to create a new version of life on Earth!

Please stop competing with each other for men. You are needed to show them the way after you have found it. You must lead this movement within your Selves so that you can be fully empowered as women to calmly and receptively be the true force that you are. Look inside for the answers. Don't look to the world to tell you which way to go. Tune in and listen to your inner voice, your intuitive voice, which will always tell you the Truth. In fact, the more you pay attention to it, the louder and clearer it will become.

I know that, for many of you, change is scary. That is why you so desperately cling to the old order and the current status quo when it comes to your relationships. You believe that it is easier to hold on to the familiar, even when that which you are used to is continuously causing you pain. But it's the known pain that you have numbed your Selves to, while you remain in fear of the unknown.

If you could just let go and take the leap of faith, I assure you that, not only will you land on your feet, you will wind up walking a path which leads to peace, joy, and ultimate fulfillment. You will be part of creating a transformed world where Unconditional Love and Acceptance reign supreme. You will attain Emotional Independence on this path of evolvement and you will come to know your Selves as never before.

When you take your proper place, no one can take it from you. It is uniquely yours alone. There will be no threat to your security. No one will be competing to take anything away from you that is your rightful place of being. From this place, you will be able to recognize your true male counterpart. He will then do the work he needs to do to become your true equal.

In this state of equality, we are free to continue evolving in the Light while we remain in the physical realm. We will be reversing the curse of the metaphorical Garden of Eden, which led to women becoming oppressed and subservient to men by the "powers that be," and we will be restoring Heaven to Earth in a way that never was before. Ascendance! Utopia! Paradise!

I know we have a little way to go before this dream can become fully manifest but, in the meantime, I strongly suggest that you begin to shift your awareness off of this world's apparent reality along with all of its intense conditioning and brainwashing, and you start putting your energy towards creating your ideal version of a perfect world. Then don't settle for less!

Know that I love each and every one of you from the depths of my Being. I send you all my Loving Light to support and guide you as you journey to Emotional Independence and True Freedom. Remember that the path of Ascension calls for your heightened awareness. May you all quickly realize your full potential and may the Goddess within each of you wake up and take charge of your life!

With Unconditional Love and Acceptance,

In Loving Light,

She Who Knows

P.S. I am here for all of you... as Creative Source Energy, as Universal Mother, as Queen of the Goddesses and, in this dimension, as Dr. Pamela, to facilitate your becoming She Who Grows ...forever and always.

From My Heart and Soul to Yours,

Dr. Pamela

Pamela M. Zimmer, Ph.D.

* * *

GRAND FINALE

Can I get a drum roll, please?

LOVE YOUR SELF THE WAY YOU DESIRE TO BE LOVED!

BECOME THE LOVE YOU ARE!

BE THE LOVE YOU SEEK!

As Gandhi has so prolifically pointed out:

"You must become the change you want to see in the world."

* * *

This is not the end. It's only...

THE BEGINNING!

* * *

APPENDIX A

ARE YOU A SABOTEUR?

I've designed a scale to help you determine if you are sabotaging yourself and your relationships, in turn. This is a great tool to help develop your self-awareness of your particular patterns when it comes to the opposite sex!

Choose a response from the scale below that best identifies your current pattern in regard to each of the following statements and note its point value:

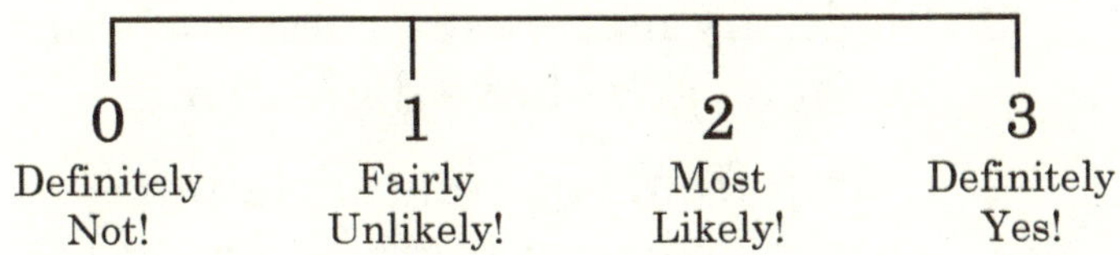

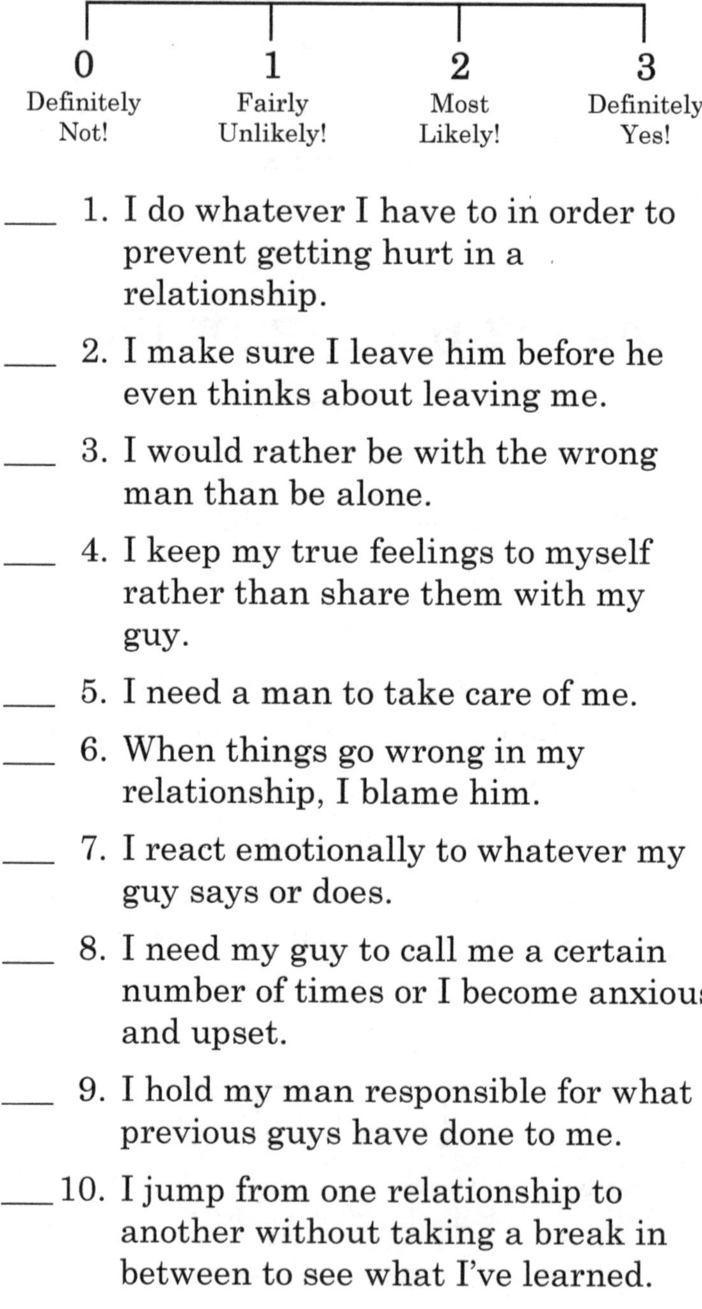

0	1	2	3
Definitely Not!	Fairly Unlikely!	Most Likely!	Definitely Yes!

___ 1. I do whatever I have to in order to prevent getting hurt in a relationship.

___ 2. I make sure I leave him before he even thinks about leaving me.

___ 3. I would rather be with the wrong man than be alone.

___ 4. I keep my true feelings to myself rather than share them with my guy.

___ 5. I need a man to take care of me.

___ 6. When things go wrong in my relationship, I blame him.

___ 7. I react emotionally to whatever my guy says or does.

___ 8. I need my guy to call me a certain number of times or I become anxious and upset.

___ 9. I hold my man responsible for what previous guys have done to me.

___ 10. I jump from one relationship to another without taking a break in between to see what I've learned.

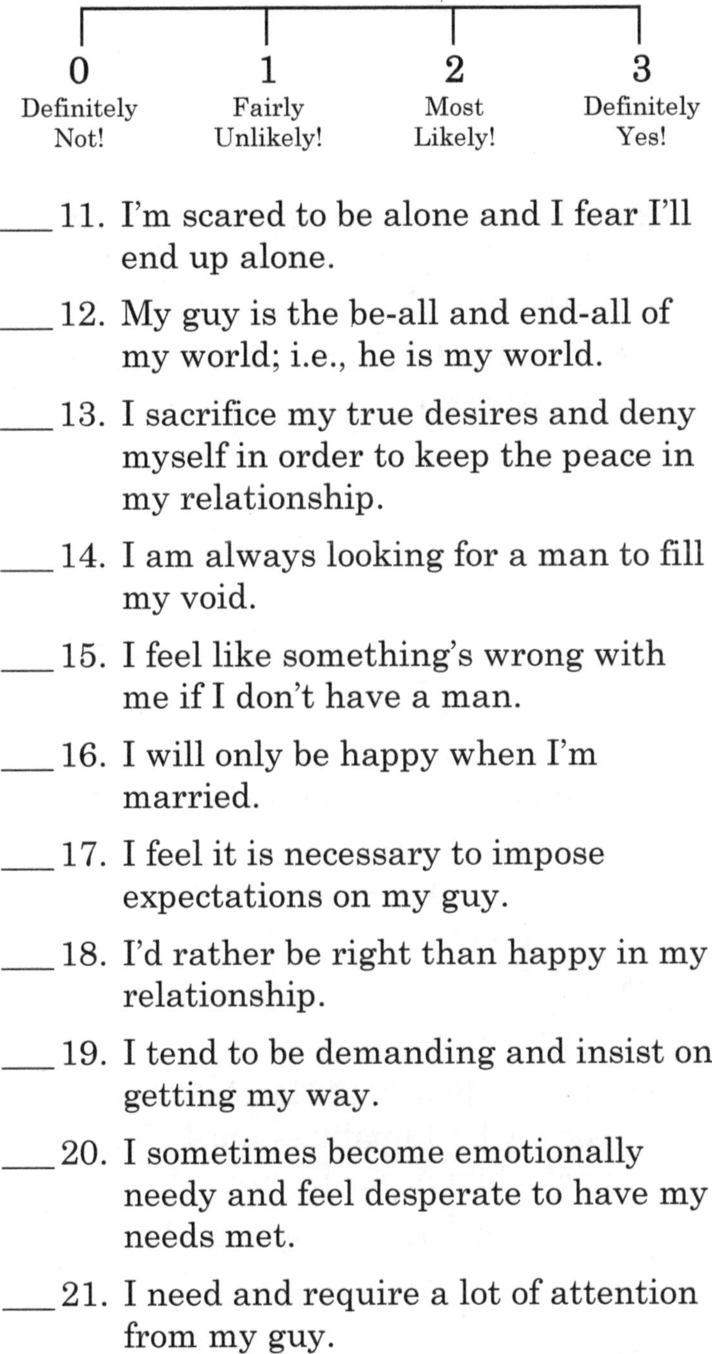

0	1	2	3
Definitely Not!	Fairly Unlikely!	Most Likely!	Definitely Yes!

___ 11. I'm scared to be alone and I fear I'll end up alone.

___ 12. My guy is the be-all and end-all of my world; i.e., he is my world.

___ 13. I sacrifice my true desires and deny myself in order to keep the peace in my relationship.

___ 14. I am always looking for a man to fill my void.

___ 15. I feel like something's wrong with me if I don't have a man.

___ 16. I will only be happy when I'm married.

___ 17. I feel it is necessary to impose expectations on my guy.

___ 18. I'd rather be right than happy in my relationship.

___ 19. I tend to be demanding and insist on getting my way.

___ 20. I sometimes become emotionally needy and feel desperate to have my needs met.

___ 21. I need and require a lot of attention from my guy.

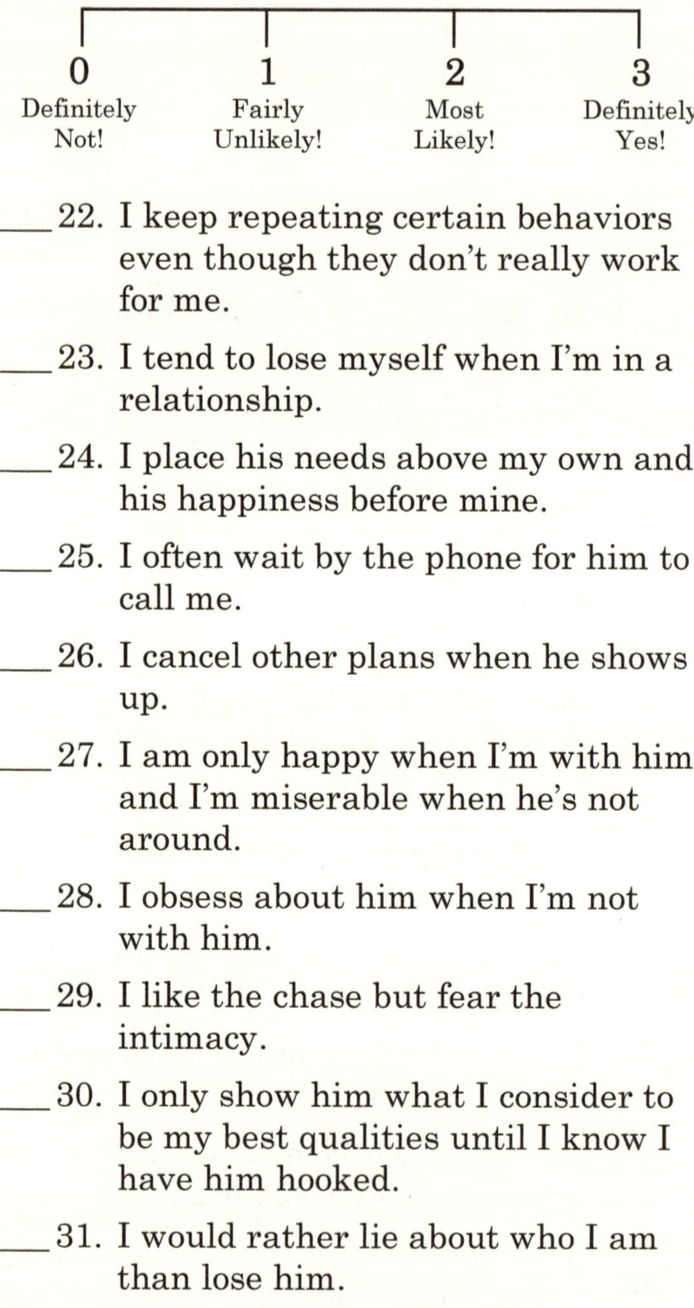

___ 22. I keep repeating certain behaviors even though they don't really work for me.

___ 23. I tend to lose myself when I'm in a relationship.

___ 24. I place his needs above my own and his happiness before mine.

___ 25. I often wait by the phone for him to call me.

___ 26. I cancel other plans when he shows up.

___ 27. I am only happy when I'm with him and I'm miserable when he's not around.

___ 28. I obsess about him when I'm not with him.

___ 29. I like the chase but fear the intimacy.

___ 30. I only show him what I consider to be my best qualities until I know I have him hooked.

___ 31. I would rather lie about who I am than lose him.

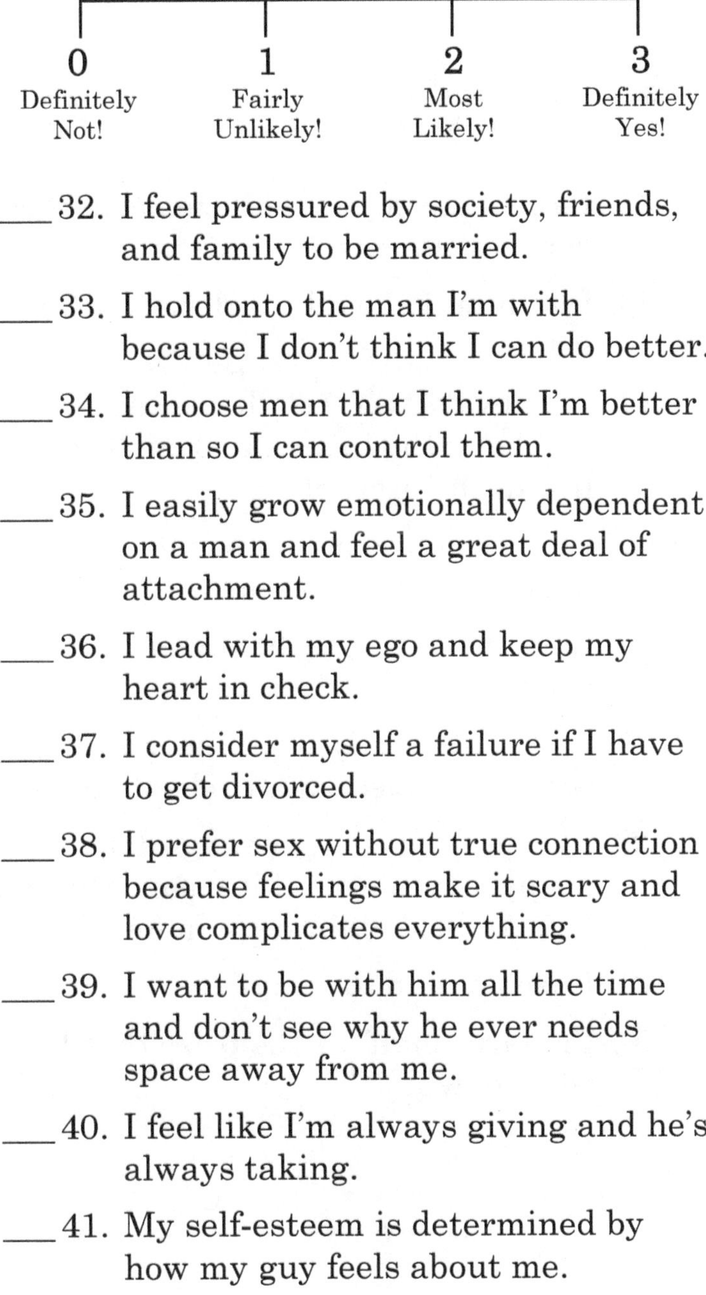

0	1	2	3
Definitely Not!	Fairly Unlikely!	Most Likely!	Definitely Yes!

___32. I feel pressured by society, friends, and family to be married.

___33. I hold onto the man I'm with because I don't think I can do better.

___34. I choose men that I think I'm better than so I can control them.

___35. I easily grow emotionally dependent on a man and feel a great deal of attachment.

___36. I lead with my ego and keep my heart in check.

___37. I consider myself a failure if I have to get divorced.

___38. I prefer sex without true connection because feelings make it scary and love complicates everything.

___39. I want to be with him all the time and don't see why he ever needs space away from me.

___40. I feel like I'm always giving and he's always taking.

___41. My self-esteem is determined by how my guy feels about me.

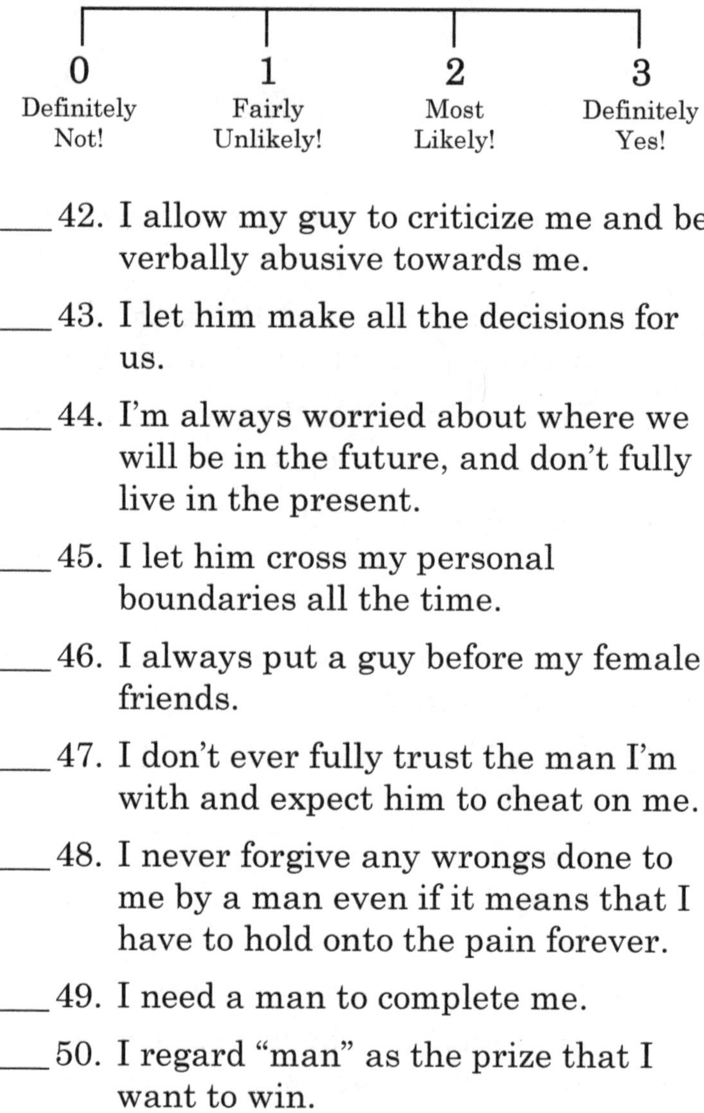

___ 42. I allow my guy to criticize me and be verbally abusive towards me.

___ 43. I let him make all the decisions for us.

___ 44. I'm always worried about where we will be in the future, and don't fully live in the present.

___ 45. I let him cross my personal boundaries all the time.

___ 46. I always put a guy before my female friends.

___ 47. I don't ever fully trust the man I'm with and expect him to cheat on me.

___ 48. I never forgive any wrongs done to me by a man even if it means that I have to hold onto the pain forever.

___ 49. I need a man to complete me.

___ 50. I regard "man" as the prize that I want to win.

* * *

RATING SCALE

Now add up the point values that you have assigned each statement. When you have your total, turn the page to check out how you are rated according to how much or how little you indulge in Self-Sabotage and Relationship Sabotage.

GRAND TOTAL _____

0 – 50 = *Wow! Congratulations! You seem to be well on your way to Emotional Independence when it comes to men. You are making conscious choices that support your growth and are remembering to honor your Self. Stay awake, stay aware, and keep on evolving!*

You appear to be containing any tendencies that you may have towards Relationship Sabotage as well as Self-Sabotage. Either that or you avoid any serious or intimate connections with the opposite sex!

P.S. I may have to recruit you as a facilitator in my global endeavor to wake women up so that they, too, start making healthy choices that are self-nurturing when it comes to the men in their lives.

*

51 – 100 = *Oops! You likely have unresolved issues from your past that affect you in your present relationships with men.*

You may feel out of control in certain areas of your life and may project those fears onto your mate. You may stop yourself from time to time from going too far, but you are inconsistent in your ability to care for your Self. In fact, you probably feel you need him to provide you with a dose of self-esteem.

You want to believe that you have a good grasp on how to behave in your relationships but you often betray your Self by denying your own Truth and desires. You are intermittently engaging in Self-Sabotage and your potential partner will likely reap the fall-out.

*

101 – 150 = *Aaagh! You are out of control! Get out of the driver's seat and take this opportunity to become a passenger on this journey. You need time and space for your Self to stop and smell the roses! You're on a treadmill going nowhere fast. You're stuck in your destructive patterns* *and are probably not even actively looking for a way out.*

You need to take a Chill Pill! If you continue in this mode, you will likely destroy whatever is left of your relationship or you will prevent yourself from ever creating a healthy relationship. My strong suggestion is that you take the time to really look at your Self and see what you may have to realize about your patterns to even begin moving out of your heavy dose of Self-Sabotage which can and will poison all of your relationships with the opposite sex!

APPENDIX B

Dr. Pamela presents...
MY RELATIONSHIP COMMANDMENTS

Words of Wisdom to Remember and Live By

- Since I teach people how to treat me, I will continually demonstrate how best to love me by always loving myself.
- Forgiving is *"for giving"* love to myself by no longer choosing pain as an option. This does not mean that I condone your behavior or that you are no longer responsible for your actions. It does mean that I let go of the pain as well as the responsibility I was taking from you and for you.

- I will not deny my truth and sacrifice myself in order to keep you content. When I compromise myself in any way, I become less than I am. This serves neither of us.
- I will share myself with you in a healthy way by always loving myself and being true to Who I Am.
- If I settle for less than I truly desire, I am broadcasting to the Universe that I am not worthy of better. This then continues to be my reality.
- My relationship continues to serve its purpose as long as both of us continue to grow and evolve as individuals. It becomes a truly healthy relationship when we can both grow in unity and harmony with each other as well.
- Everyday I will look at my reflection in the mirror and remind myself of the love I contain and feel for my true Self. This daily reminder will serve to center me and open my heart so that I make healthier choices for myself and for my relationship.
- I will not give my power away and make myself less than what I am. This not only makes you more important than me, but also leaves me powerless and feeling like a victim.

- I must always remember that I am powerful; I am fabulous; I am filled with Light, and I emanate love, because I am Love.
- If I lose myself in order to prevent losing you, I have actually won nothing and lost everything.
- I will believe in my Self and in my worthiness to receive the best. I will fully allow what I truly desire to flow to me and will remain in a receptive state to let it flow through me.
- Make no mistake about it… I AM WOMAN and I've come to be the Light and shine my Light upon you… if you are worthy of me!
- I will not accept any treatment that is abusive in nature or demeans me in any way. You will not project your fears, insecurities or inadequacies upon me.
- I will rise up to my full stature and take the position that is my true place and my Divine birthright. My Soul Self will support me in this. The Universe will cheer.
- I am responsible for me and for preserving my Truth. I will not blame you for that which is mine to fix and change.
- All change begins with me. I must become the change I want to see reflected in my relationship.

All this... or even better!

So be it!

* * *

MY CONTRACTUAL AGREEMENT

I hereby agree to receive and apply the above terms to myself on a daily basis and thus empower myself to be All That I AM!

With Love From and To My Self,

____

Your Signature

Contact Dr. Pamela

For further information on other ways you can learn to create and grow healthy relationships and/or to be informed of future events, publications, recordings, broadcasts, public appearances, speaking engagements, Q and A workshops, e-mail:

drpamela@growinghealthyrelationships.com

* * *

To order an audio version of ***Sex, Lies and Sabotage*** – a CD recording of Dr. Pamela reading her book, e-mail:

drpamela@sexliesandsabotage.com

* * *

To read additional articles written by Dr. Pamela, visit her blog site at:

www.growinghealthyrelationships.com

www.ingramcontent.com/pod-product-compliance
Lightning Source LLC
LaVergne TN
LVHW091642100826
845152LV00006B/137/J
9780578010786